THE ART
OF HEALING
AND MANIFESTING

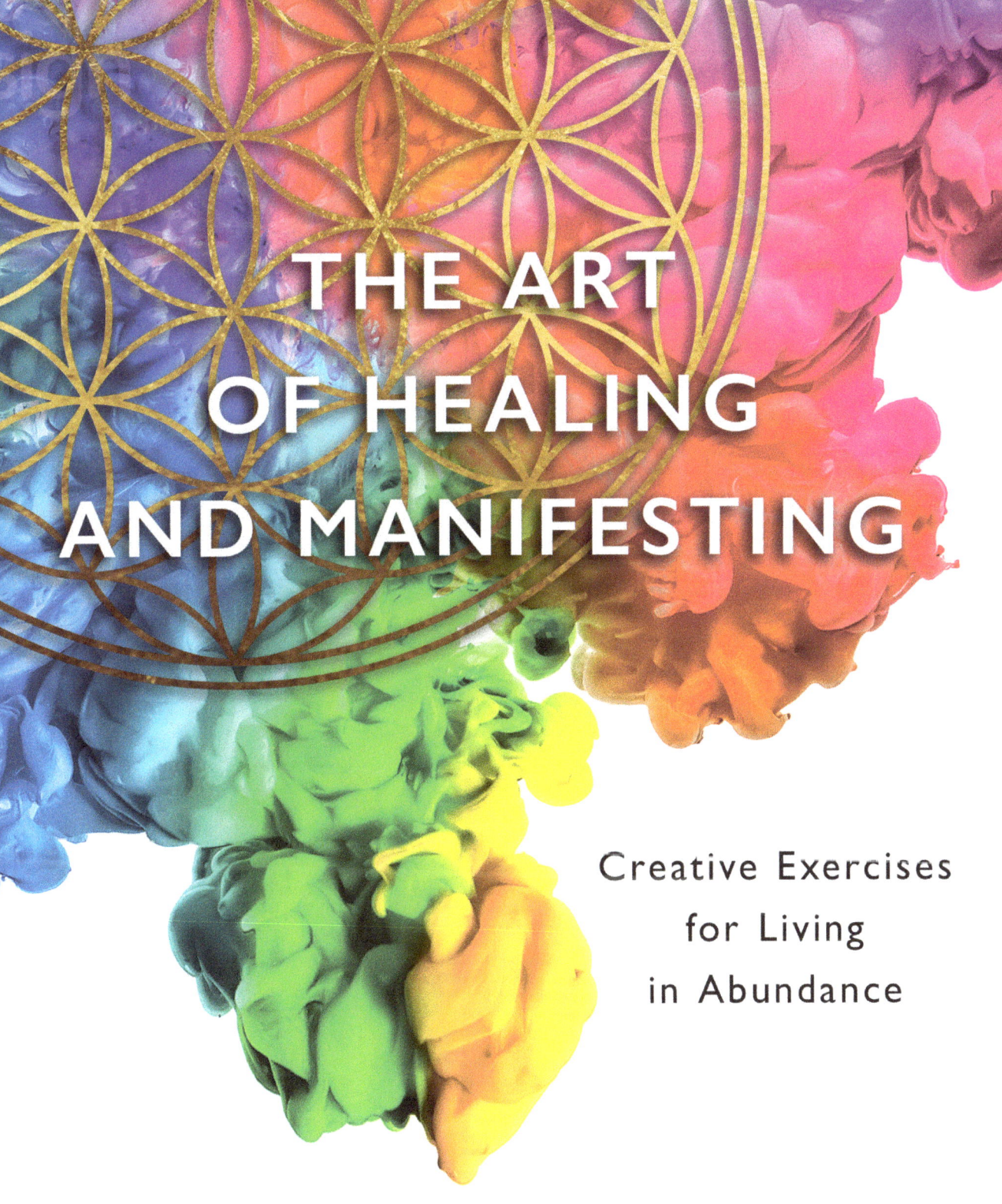

Copyrighted Material

The Art of Healing and Manifesting: Creative Exercises for Living in Abundance

Copyright © 2022 by Leah Guzman. All Rights Reserved.

No part of this publication may be reproduced, stored in a retrieval system or transmitted, in any form or by any means—electronic, mechanical, photocopying, recording or otherwise—without prior written permission from the publisher, except for the inclusion of brief quotations in a review.

For information about this title or to order other books and/or electronic media, contact the publisher:

Leah Guzman
www.leahguzman.com
hello@leahguzman.com

ISBNs:
978-1-7379202-0-5 (softcover)
978-1-7379202-1-2 (eBook)

Printed in the United States of America

Cover and Interior design: 1106 Design

Nonfiction, Self-Help, Art Therapy, Art Techniques, Chakras, Law of Attraction, Manifesting, Psychology and Counseling, Mental Health, Medical Psychology, Crafts, Hobbies and Home Arts, Photography, Alternative Medicine, Art Therapy, and Relaxation Medicine

This book is dedicated to my daughter, Carmen,
in case she needs a road map on her creative journey in life.

CONTENTS

Introduction	ix
CHAPTER 1	
Crown Chakra: Connecting to Consciousness	1
CHAPTER 2	
Third Eye Chakra: Listen to Your Intuition	21
CHAPTER 3	
Throat Chakra: Communication and Creativity	47
CHAPTER 4	
Heart Chakra: Giving and Receiving Love	67
CHAPTER 5	
Solar Plexus: Building Willpower and Purpose	91
CHAPTER 6	
Sacral Chakra: Letting Go to Let Joy In	115
CHAPTER 7	
Root Chakra: Surviving to Thriving	133
Acknowledgments	157
References	161
About the Author	163

OPENING MIND, BODY AND SOUL THROUGH ART

INTRODUCTION

*H*ello, **Creative Soul! Congratulations!** You have decided to answer the call and listen to your soul. My intention for writing this book is to share the tools I've been using as an art therapist and artist to create my own abundant, happy life as well as my clients'. I truly believe art is my superpower. Art has been there to help me during the most challenging times in my life and manifesting the most beautiful experiences. The process in this book is a mix of reflecting, making, and co-creating with the Universe for direction. Everything in life is connected. We are energetic beings. I've had the privilege of working as an art therapist and teaching effective tools to hundreds of individuals. In turn, they have been able to level up their life as well.

I'm excited for you to use this as a guide on your journey. Take it at your own pace. You can follow along the path of art exercises and see how each creation is interconnected. You will also learn how your art has a message for you. This art-making process connects you to your higher self. Art has a language, and your intuition is speaking to you. You will learn how to use this practice to help you heal emotional wounds and use art as a way to manifest your desires. This is an opportunity for you to show up confidently in your practice and share your gifts with the world. Let's get started!

> *"If you're going to live, leave a legacy.*
> *Make a mark on the world that can't be erased."*
> ~ MAYA ANGELOU

INTRODUCTION xi

How to Use This Book

I'm delighted to start this voyage with you. Grab your favorite journal, and gather your art supplies. Let's see what's on the horizon for you. The fact that you are reading this book right now means your intuition has led you here. The purpose of this book is to manifest your desires using art techniques that can help you change your energy and how you move through the world. I will share the sacred wisdom of the ancient Hindu philosophy of the Chakra system, which is based on energy. We will also explore the Law of Attraction and how our own energy will reflect what is showing up in our reality. My favorite part about using the art processes that I include in this book is to see your transformation and "Aha's!" as they show up in your life. The underlying intention here is to nurture your creativity, feel good through the process, and tap into your soul's desire to experience everything you want in your life. This is an exciting journey! These techniques will give you insight into what your soul wants to experience and clarity for reaching your specific life desires.

The Universe gives us our own unique gifts as well as desires you want to experience. What do you want to bring in? Whether it's to create an art series, have your work in museums, write a book, have a successful creative business, manifest a lover, experience happiness, or level up your life in some way, this book will give you an opportunity to creatively align and recalibrate your energy to manifest it. The exercises are deep dives to get clear on what you want and to raise your vibration along the way to attract your desire. Schedule your time to work on the healing exercises, focusing on balancing your lowest scores from the Chakra test. You can do each exercise that feels well-aligned for you. Once you've done the healing work, move onto the manifesting, and follow the prompts. The intention of this book is to nurture your creativity as you are stepping into your desires. Art is a powerful tool for healing and manifesting.

This book is designed to guide you in healing the wounds that have stopped you from showing up as your most authentic self. It will guide you in creative exercises to self-reflect, create new avenues of abundance, manifest your desires, and listen to your soul's calling. Your soul wants to experience life. It's not always an easy path. It's more like the (s)hero's journey of a winding labyrinth with twists and turns, getting lost, and finding yourself again. You will see from the artist interviews the darkest times as well as the contrasts, bring in the richness of life. It's about embracing the darkness and cultivating your energy to experience the goodness, too. Have fun with the prompts. The art directives give guidance as challenges arise.

The most important part of the process is setting aside time for nurturing your creativity. When will you have the time? Most creatives tend to lack the structure necessary to implement the tools that will kickstart their creative flow. Start by setting up a schedule that works for you. For example, I get up an hour earlier than anyone in my house to meditate, art journal, and exercise. Setting aside fifteen-minute segments helps me get a clear mind to start my day. I started this practice after going way too long racing out the door with anxiety to get my kids to school on time. Who wants to start their day in a whirlwind? Not me. The practices in this book can be done as part of a daily routine as well. Pick a time in your day when you can consistently show up for daily self-care. If you dedicate seven weeks to implement the tools, you will see transformation. If you fall off from creating, recommit, and begin again.

According to clinical psychiatrist Dr. Dan Siegel, who teaches about healthy minds, the brain needs to have seven experiences throughout your day for it to perform optimally. Every area of your life will be touched upon in this book, because everything in life is interconnected. The seven experiences are: sleep time, connection time (social interaction), exercise time, down time, focused time, time in (meditation), and play time. As I mentioned, you will review every area of your life to level up. You can use the principles to balance out your day. If you can create one successful day in which you have balanced your energy, it will lead to a successful life. Sleep time is getting adequate rest. Connection time is bonding with others. Exercise can be simply to move your body. Down time is being present and observing what is in front of you. Down time is simple being, sitting, and observing nature. Focused time relates to work and concentrating. Time in is related to meditation, guided examples of which I will give you in this book. Play time is allowing yourself to have fun. Is there one area of your life that may need more attention? This is an opportunity to look at how you structure your time and include more breaks. The techniques in this book can be used for your play time, down time, or time in. When I give myself time to experience each of the principles, I feel a sense of satisfaction in my day. Most of my friends ask me, "How do you accomplish so much with your time?" It's really being able to balance my energy to give each area attention.

Practicing the exercises in this book will give you a series of Chakra-inspired paintings, tools for healing, and ways to shape your dreams through creative practice. I've created many Chakra sets throughout the years. I've sold these activated art pieces, gifted them, and continue to use this process as a way to manifest. If you are questioning, this process will help you gain clarity on your practice and how to use art intentionally for co-creation with Source. You have this amazing opportunity to connect with Source daily ("God," "The Universe"—whatever resonates). An important part of nurturing this inner journey is to know that you're never alone. You are being supported.

We may feel that we are on a certain path and nurturing our own gardens. Yet, you will be visiting villages and cities where other creatives thrive. One group of like-minded friends is the online Facebook group Creative Soul Online Retreat. This is a community for you to ask questions and share your journey's treasures. We are all here for you and to support each other. You are welcome to join us.

Benefits of this book

- Create Chakra mandala drawings for setting your intentions
- A collection of Chakra art, set with activated symbols and colors
- Uncover your blocks and limited beliefs
- Find your superpower and unique gifts you offer the world
- Learn how to use your intuition as a guiding tool
- Co-create with The Universe
- Road map created by your Higher Self for your next best steps
- Connect with like-minded creatives
- Get into the Creative Flow
- Manifest your desires
- Feel like a badass because you did it!

As creatives, we provide the world with what it needs. Art is what shapes society. We're very powerful beings, and we've got to keep showing up and sharing our gifts.

Therapeutic Art for Healing and Manifesting

Art allows you to visually see your thoughts in front of you through reflective distancing. Everything you create is an extension of yourself. This book will give you therapeutic art exercises to explore how to heal the energy (feelings) associated with a certain area of your life. What I have observed in my art therapy practice is that many people want to manifest *more* of something (better health, happier relationships, money, or satisfying work). For example: You're wanting more money for a bigger house or to sponsor a charity, and you feel blocked. It's an opportunity to explore your own story and the energy that is holding you back. If you are wanting a lover, it's important to look at your own self-love. Many times, we tend to ignore our own story. We need to explore parts of ourselves that are blocking the manifesting process. Once you have done the inner work—exploring past traumas, triggers (things that set you off)—then you can get into the frequency of what you want, and the manifesting process becomes fun. Life goes more smoothly. We will be assessing every area of your life. Everything in life is a relationship. It's important to look at each relationship you have with time, spirituality, family, partners, friends, finances, nature, and—most importantly—yourself.

Healing Time

When my children were small—my son was around four, and my daughter was one—I was practicing art therapy full time; all my needs were being met, except for one. We had a home, and we were financially secure; we had love and our health. Yet, I was missing an essential ingredient. I was experiencing bouts of depression and high anxiety. Why was I waking up in the middle of the night trying to process what had happened in the day? Literally, I would find myself in the bathroom at 3:00 a.m. crying and scribbling in my journal. It was a wake-up call that I was experiencing burnout. I wasn't taking care of my own needs. My self-care was non-existent. I was a people pleaser, saying "Yes" to everyone who asked me to do something. I put *everyone else* first. Not knowing how to say "No" got me in a hole that I didn't know how to get out of. Sometimes you can't always get out of a hole on your own. I had a visual of me in a hole, yelling from the bottom, "Hello—is anyone up there?"

Thank goodness I practiced my own advice and sought help from a trained art therapist. This amazing being helped me create boundaries and achieve clarity about what is really important to me. It came out in my art that I wanted a studio, to create art and share it with the world. Wow, the dark night of my soul had a great message for me to hear. This is when I created my first art-therapy book, *Rad is Smad!!!*, about a monster truck who learned how to deal with his sad and mad feelings. Looking back on it, what I was doing was processing my own feelings around not taking care of my needs, holding resentment, and refusing to get help. I'm definitely the kind of person who likes to take care of things on my own. So, learning to surrender and seek support was a huge step for me. When I took the time to process those emotions and realize what my soul wanted, everything shifted. If you need someone to hold space for you to process your emotions, then I highly recommend investing in support. You deserve it!

The benefits of taking the time for self-care and nurturing your garden (mind) will be bountiful. Research shows that making art allows you to reframe experiences, reorganize thoughts, and gain personal insights that enhance your quality of life. Making art specifically related to your life helps you analyze current situations so you can make good choices for your future. One of the other great benefits of creating art is that research shows it reduces cortisol levels (the stress hormone). This is why making it a daily habit or a few times a week can greatly impact your well-being.

Manifesting Time

As I did the healing work, it helped me gain clarity around what I really wanted. I remember writing down a detailed list of what I wanted in a house—a pool, an extra bedroom for a studio, and a big yard for the kids to play in. I created this drawing in my sessions. Magically, The Universe aligned, and I received this gift. It was an awakening for me that, as I heal, just like I assist others in doing, my clients can manifest their desires, too. The Universe continues to share this process with me.

As you work through this book, you will see a repeated pattern of mandalas, affirmations, meditations, and Chakra paintings. These are for grounding you into seeing how everything is interconnected. This is a creative practice that nurtures your soul. This process isn't a one-time quick fix. It's a creative lifestyle of being intentional to bring in your desires, of opening a portal to your creativity and your superpower. The meditations allow you to listen. Your mandalas will hold affirmations and intentions. Your Chakra art will hold symbolism. It will be a compass on your path. Art is a gateway to Source.

Science supports nurturing creativity to improve mental health and every other area of your life. Creating art can rewire your brain's plasticity, which allows for you to be more flexible and adaptable. Engaging in any sort of visual expression results in the reward pathway in the brain being activated. Research shows blood flows to this part of the brain to trigger the feeling of satisfaction and pleasure. Making art allows you to experience the "flow" state. "Flow" is characterized by increased theta-wave activity in the frontal areas of the brain—and moderate alpha-wave activities in the frontal and central areas. As you use these art-manifesting techniques, you'll be opening avenues to more opportunities and abundance.

Meditations

You will find pre-recorded meditations in the resource portal on my site. As a part of my daily practice, I start off with meditating to settle my mind, in order to receive guidance from Source. Structure and consistency in your creative practice are crucial. Quieting your mind to focus will help you start your art. Once you are able to settle, just as in meditation, it allows you to get into the "Zone of Creating." The benefits of meditation are numerous. You'll find yourself carrying the calmness with you throughout the day. Once you start, you won't want to stop. I have a consistent morning routine, in which I drink water with lemon, meditate, write my morning pages, and then go for a walk. This gives my fertile mind an opportunity to clear the weeds (clutter) in my head and call in my priorities for the day. It's a direct opportunity to be guided by Source. I must mention that I wake up at 5:00 a.m. in order to make this happen. It's when everything is still. If this is something new for you, begin by using the pre-recorded meditations that I offer you as a gift on my site. You can use the meditations and visualizations over and over as a way to go deeper into the process. https://leahguzman.com/resource-guide. Use this as an opportunity to experiment to see what happens to your energy throughout the day as you practice these techniques.

Mandalas

Mandala means "circle" in Sanskrit. The mandala is a container for holding emotions and symbols. It's a design that radiates from the center and is often seen in art, architecture, and throughout nature. It's been used as a ritual, religious symbolism, and as a drawing medium to center and integrate your "higher self." We are using it specifically to identify our desires and infuse our affirmations to activate the art in healing and manifesting. The mandala directive is the starting point for the healing journey in this book.

Affirmations

Affirmations are declarations of your desires. The affirmations that you incorporate into your art can be utilized as a way to strengthen the Chakras and your beliefs. This will also be a way to get clear with your intentions. Repeated affirmations can change the subconscious mind into believing what you desire (in case you had any doubts). I like to infuse the affirmations into the mandalas created in my journal. You will learn a very special technique to clear your limited beliefs with the affirmations.

Coloring Pages

The beginning chapter images in the book can be used as coloring pages. As you complete each coloring page, you will have a beautiful rainbow to flip through. The actual images are downloadable as well on my site at https://leahguzman.com/product/downloadable-chakra-drawings.

Chakra Sets

The Chakra sets offer you an opportunity to paint and use symbolism to strengthen the energy centers in your body. Each painting also is set with an intention of what you want to heal or manifest related to your desire. I like to call this "activated art." Each Chakra has a color frequency, emotional correlation, animals for guidance, elements in nature, and association to life situations. This process infuses creating seven paintings associated with each Chakra. The best part is that you will end up with a beautiful collection of seven Chakra paintings infused with your energy, which will look divine when you hang them up. Once you complete the set, it creates a rainbow when it is all lined up. This will be hung up on a wall, so you can see them on a daily basis. When I first started exhibiting my work, I included the Chakra sets. I found it so interesting how many people were interested in them, even if they didn't know about the Chakras. They were always attracting people—the rainbow colors resonate at a certain frequency that magnetizes the feeling of joy.

Interviews

The interviews are from seasoned artists and manifestors who are following the principles of the Law of Attraction and have successfully mastered bringing in their desires. Each person shares their tools, challenges, and words of wisdom to support you on your journey. Many nuggets of wisdom are offered. The participants were guest speakers in the Creative Soul Society Membership.

Spirit Guides

A part of this process of co-creating with The Universe is calling on support. This may take the shape of asking angels, spirit guides, people, or animals. We use animal symbols throughout the Chakra sets. Each Chakra has associated animals and symbols to guide us on our path.

Questions for Reflection:

In each exercise, there are questions for you to reflect on. Take the time to write out your answers in your journal. Going deeper in reflection helps you get clearer on what really serves you.

Creative Soul Online Retreat Community

The Creative Soul Online Retreat is a growing Facebook community to connect with like-minded souls. You have the opportunity to share your art created from this book about your journey of healing and manifesting. If you prefer to create art alongside fellow creatives during online monthly meetups you can join us in the Creative Soul Society Membership group.

Material List

- Art Journal
- Daily Planner (online or paper version)
- Pencil
- Assorted drawing media: Colored pencils, gel pens, or markers
- Black ink pen
- Seven small canvases (4" x 4") or (6" x 6")

- Images inspired by or found on the Internet

- Acrylic paint (black, white, gold, shades of red, orange, yellow, green, blue, purple)

- Brushes

- Water container

- Paper towel

Manifesting and the Law of Attraction

My first experience with the concept of the Law of Attraction was the Oprah Winfrey interview with Esther Hicks, also known as Abraham. I was fascinated to learn that, through her meditation practice (also known as channeling) she was able to receive direct messages from Source, and she was able to answer questions to assist others on their journey. I got hooked on listening to her Youtube recordings. I read every book, and I realized that, every time I listened to her, I felt the high frequency of love. When you are connected to Source energy, that is what you feel. Any time you are in a lower vibration, you have lost the connection. The tools in this book will help you tune back in to getting connected, also known as alignment for manifesting your desires easily. Many of the concepts she discussed were about the inner feeling (energy) that you experience will show up in your physical reality.

    I found it fascinating, because the concept directly related to my knowledge in cognitive-behavioral art therapy. Your thoughts (cognitions), create feelings, which, in turn, manifest behaviors. The process of the Law of Attraction is really about becoming conscious of your thought processes and weeding your garden, in order to align your energy (feelings) to what you desire in life. The concepts are parallel. Those who have practiced this for a while know that the results can be fascinating! If you are just starting out, see it as an experiment. Have fun using the art techniques to identify your emotions. You will be giving your energy the attention it deserves. You may need healing to balance your energy (if it's stuck). There are many different ways to balance your energy. I recommend using several methods and art as a way to activate the energy flow. On the other hand, if your energy is already in alignment, you will create your desire through the art-making and manifesting process.

Be a Vibrational Match

"The Universe knows all things and is responding to the vibration that you are sending. When you are sending your vibration on purpose, you are orchestrating what The Universe is aligning for you."
~ Esther Hicks

Resistance and Limiting Beliefs

Resistance shows up in our lives when we need healing. If you're struggling in an area, this is a sign to go deeper. It's not necessarily a negative place to be when you feel stuck or blocked. It's an opportunity to grow. Resistance may show up as a feeling of anxiety, frustration, complacency, or anger. It shows up in our lives as obstacles to getting what we want. It's when you feel stuck and can't move forward. To ignore the feeling only amplifies the situation. The same situation will continue to show up in your life until you learn the lesson. This is an opportunity to explore the feeling more, embrace it, accept it, and let it flow through you to release it. We will identify the problems that arise in each Chakra, so that you can see where you need to focus your attention. Resistance is a sign that you may need to use specific strategies to heal a situation. If something isn't working out, you can change the energy within (mentally get a new perspective) or physically change the situation. It may sound easy to do, but it takes a lot of courage and self-compassion to self-reflect. The art techniques in this book will help you explore it further. It's totally normal to feel resistance. It's part of the process. As you place your big dreams out into the world, things show up that need to be addressed. Expect them, and deal with them as they come up. For success in your manifesting process, deal with the obstacles head on.

Limiting beliefs are at the base of your psyche and subconscious mind. When we want something and find that there is a block that keeps showing up, then you have to identify your limiting belief. When I first started offering my art for sale and my online art-therapy services, I really wanted to make money and be compensated for my time. Yet, I had money shame. What is money shame? Well, at the time, I knew I wanted more money, yet I didn't know that, energetically, I was pushing it away. I had to understand that I needed to feel worthy to receive and become more intimate with my finances. At the time, I was scared to visit my tax person and even open my bills. Energetically, I was pushing away money. One of my first coaches had me video tape myself ripping up a dollar bill. I was shocked to see myself freak out about ripping a piece of paper. You can give the dollar to the bank, and they will give you a new one. This exercise made me aware that I had subconscious beliefs that I was unaware of and needed to address.

At the same time, I realized the energy I had for money was anxiety. When someone asked how much my art or art-therapy services were, I would cringe. Money was something that I had associated with fear. I learned that I had this limiting belief that stemmed from childhood. One of my first money stories was related to a time in my life when I had to move from my hometown because of "money." This triggered a turbulent time in my teenage years, associated with depression. The upside was that art was my outlet. I hadn't processed the emotions from what had happened in my youth. When I made the connection of why I associated money with fear and anxiety, I got in touch with my money monster. I was then able to heal the wound, and the Universe gifted me. When I made the inner connection and explored my shame to heal the wounds, the very next day, I sold a thousand-dollar painting. I felt the shift, and it was exciting! Most of our limiting beliefs are from the past, handed down from our parents and teachers. We aren't aware that what they are instilling in our mind isn't a fit for us. When we grow up, we can tend to our garden better. You might have an amazing mango tree planted, yet you're allergic to mangos. Look at what beliefs you have around what it is that you want to manifest and see if there is something there that is stopping you.

Limiting beliefs can also stem from a negative experience. Maybe we failed at something, or it didn't go the way we expected? I invite you to take some time now and find out your own story. What area in your life are you feeling stuck about? Go ahead and write your story to find those limiting beliefs.

I invite you to slow down to do the inner work; give yourself space and time to heal. If you're feeling stuck, sense that you're blocked, or are experiencing doubts, then focus on the healing exercises. Our inner-feeling system, also known as our intuition, is designed to guide you to feel your way into moving in the direction of feeling good and manifesting. There are times when we can do it on our own, and I give examples in this book.

Yet, there are also times when seeking help will catapult your process. If you are experiencing a limiting belief caused by a traumatic event in your life (past abuse, neglect, or grief), then I recommend seeking support from a trained art therapist. Meeting with a trained therapist allows you the opportunity to explore where and how you're stuck in certain patterns of behavior. If you have been suffering for some time (in a hole, like the one I mentioned earlier), then you may have limiting beliefs that you would need support with to help address your patterns of thinking. Feelings such as shame will take time to reprogram. A trained art therapist will provide a container into which you can put those feelings and achieve reflective distancing. You can step away, see the situation from a new perspective, and make space for processing your emotions. The safe container that the art therapist provides assists in your transformation. If you're not conscious of your beliefs, it makes it difficult to question them and see life in a new way. The therapeutic process allows you to understand your beliefs (created from past experiences) and then retrain your brain for new ones.

One of the most common questions I get asked is, 'Why would I seek help from a trained art therapist or coach?" Because sometimes you are unaware that the experiences that you have had in your childhood have conditioned your mind. Getting support will speed up your healing process to a few months rather than suffering through several years. Therapy also offers you a different perspective in order for you to achieve reflective distancing to see how you've been conditioned, how your past experiences have shaped your current reality. It helps you connect the dots. Once you are able to free yourself from the limiting beliefs, it will ease you into manifesting as a lifestyle.

You deserve only the best. Whether you decide to do your healing on your own or with support, there is no judgment. This book is a tool with nuggets of wisdom through the interviews, guided art directives, and the signs you are receiving from The Universe.

Chakra Overview

The Chakras, also known as energy centers in the body, are spinning wheels that have a frequency. *Chakra* means "wheel of energy." The Chakra philosophy originated 2000 years ago. Each Chakra vibrates at a certain frequency and color. I see them like a portal, relating to our emotions, the body, our relationships, elements in The Universe, and how our lives function. Being in balance allows you to be in the "flow" state. When all the wheels are spinning at a balanced frequency, you will feel in the flow of life. Manifesting your desires will come easily to you. Synchronicity will show up consistently. When you are in this state, The Universe provides signs, and you feel guided, supported. Balanced energy feels harmonious and joyful, and elevates your well-being.

However, life happens and events (small and large) can imbalance us. Our Chakras will end up spinning too fast or too slow. My intention for this book is to explore each Chakra and how it pertains to your life. This *process* is about feeling good and learning different life lessons that make life beautiful. There is beauty in contrast. When events don't go our way, that doesn't mean it's negative—it's an opportunity for growth. We are looking for the lesson.

How do we know if we are off balance? You can feel it. Resistance sneaks in, and you feel bothered. These are signs that you have to do the inner work in order to see a change on the outside. Healing and becoming balanced requires a range of different techniques. I've included a variety of tools with an emphasis on art as a way to heal. We first identify where we are feeling resistance, pain, or being "stuck" in our life. We use the body-mapping image to see which Chakra correlates and do the exercises related to moving the energy.

I was inspired to write this book because it was a point in my life when I was experiencing high anxiety, wasn't grounded, and needed root-Chakra healing. At that time, I really needed to level up my self-care. I took the necessary steps to manage my anxiety. I had to look at every area of my life. I needed to look at my relationships with money, my body, and my creative practice. I had to do the most work in the root and solar-plexus Chakra. At that time in my life, I unconsciously decorated my home with red items. I had a red rug, and matching pillows and curtains. It was my intuition drawn to the colors that would also support my healing. As I dove deeper to understanding the techniques associated, I started to see the same connections in my clients' art and life.

I also had a "yellow" room in my house, to support the solar plexus chakra. The more I learned about the Chakras and used various art techniques to balance these Chakras, the more my anxiety was reduced. I was able to get grounded and started to bring my big dreams to life. This is also the time I started incorporating the Chakra knowledge into my art-therapy practice, to help others in their healing journey. This book is an invitation to explore different aspects of your life. I adapted Judith Anodea's "Wheels of Life" Chakra quiz that you can use on your computer to check yourself. Be honest about how you are feeling, and use the assessment as a starting point on this journey.

I recommend completing the Chakra quiz online to see where you are imbalanced. Go to that section of the book to practice the healing exercises. After you complete the healing exercise, then follow the prompts for manifesting, starting with the Crown Chakra, and work your way down to the Root Chakra.

You can start by doing a free Chakra self-test here.
https://leahguzman.com/Chakra-quiz

Many creatives whom I have surveyed and whose Chakra quiz I have reviewed tend to get stuck in the lower three Chakras (root, sacral, and solar plexus). Creatives tend to live in the dreamy idea world (third eye) and have difficulty bringing their ideas down to earth (root). Our beliefs, habits, and conditioning have come from our parents and teachers. So, we have to take the time to see where we are stuck in order to shift the energy. The root Chakra is related to our basic needs—money, family, home, and the body. As you learn the tools to take better self-care of your body, finances, relationships, and home, you will shift the energy to bring in more abundance. Many creatives will think they just want more money by selling their art. Yes, that *will* happen! Yet, there may need to be balancing in the root (addressing your relationship to money), the sacral (finding pleasure in your creations), and the solar plexus (having the confidence to boldly share your work with the world).

Color Frequency

Color is the form through which we perceive light. Color carries psychological effects. Red, which psychologically stimulates the heart and nervous system, is also associated with aggressive and initiatory energies—anger, blood, beginnings of things. Blues, by contrast, are associated with peace and tranquility, and have that effect on people. (Judith Anodea, 1987)

After taking the assessment, the lowest score is where you need to focus. Wear clothes of the color of the Chakra that you most need help in healing. Have you thought about which colors you are attracted to right now? When you connect with the color you are attracted to, you can see how it can benefit you and relate to a certain emotion. Other ways to use the color for healing is painting walls in your living space, adding decorative elements in your space (curtains, pillows), coloring the pages in this book, and carrying the associated colored crystals.

Movement of Energy in the Chakras

The energy moving from the Crown Chakra to the Root Chakra is in constant flow. It moves down and back up an energetic pathway, called Prana. Prana energy enters the body in two streams, like a battery with a positive pole (Pingala, masculine) and a negative pole (Ida, feminine). Prana circulates through the body in a system of Nadis (meridians). The Nadis and Chakras are located in the etheric body, connecting heaven and earth energies. When energy moves up your body, it's called a "current of liberation." The energy moves from Root to Crown, called *mukti* in Sanskrit. When the energy is moving up our body, it is expressing and healing. The energy moving down the body is called the "current of manifestation." The ancient masters called it *bhukti* (meaning "enjoyment") (Anodea, Lions 2012). When the energy is derived from Source—let's say an idea of inspiration, then it is moving down to be manifested here on Earth in your reality.

The energy flows up and down. The objective is to keep the flow moving in a balanced way. In the philosophy of the Chakras, when imbalance occurs, it could lead to physical ailments. Similar to Abraham Maslow's Hierarchy of Needs theory, the root chakra starts with our basic needs, moving up to our desires, belonging, and then self-actualization.

Healing and Manifesting Energy Flow of the Chakras

The chakra energy moving up your body is the "current of liberation." Deepak Chopra explains the concept of how the Law of Pure Potentiality governs the chakras. In the mukti flow, current of liberation, you receive nourishment from the earth; your roots are grounded in the root chakra. As you move up to the second sacral chakra, your creative juices are flowing. The third Chakra is empowering your intentions in the solar plexus. Next, your heart is open and exchanging love to those around you, and the connections support you with your desires in the heart chakra. Expressing your needs is in the throat chakra. The third eye chakra becomes attuned to your inner voice, intuition. Lastly, the energy moves to the crown chakra of connection with Source and spirituality.

As the energy moves down the chakras, it's referred to as the "current of manifestion," also know as *bhukti*. It's fun to bring your big dreams into reality. In the crown chakra you are co-creating with the Universe (receives downloads and inspiration). In the third-eye chakra, you are using your imagination to visualize your soul's calling, or big dream. In the throat chakra, you are speaking your desires to others. In the heart chakra you are cultivating relationships to support the desire. In the solar plexus chakra, you believe in yourself and build your confidence to take action. In the sacral chakra, you have fun creating the big vision. Lastly, in the root chakra, you are bringing that big dream into reality from creating structure and prioritizing your dream.

Manifesting with the Chakras

CHAKRAS	COLOR	LOCATION	ELEMENT
CROWN	Violet White Gold	Crown of Head	Thought
THIRD EYE	Indigo	Brow	Light
THROAT	Blue	Throat	Sound
HEART	Green	Heart Center	Air
SOLAR PLEXUS	Yellow	Solar Plexus	Fire
SACRAL	Orange	Pelvis Sacrum	Water
ROOT	Red	Perineum Base of Tailbone	Earth

MAIN FOCUS	BALANCED	BLOCKED MALFUNCTION
Connection to Spirit and Wisdom	Unity, Wisdom, Awareness, Intelligence, Miracles, Bliss	Earthly Attachments (letting go), Depression
Clear Perspective and Psychic Abilities	Clairvoyance, Intuition, Dreams, Insight, Perception, Vision	Illusion of Separation (everything is connected)
Self Expression and Life Purpose	Truth, Purpose, Expression, Artistry, Service, Communication	Lies we tell ourselves
Love and Connection	Love, Trust, Healing, Surrender, Compassion, Connection	Grief, Disconnection
Power and Identity	Power, Confidence, Strong Will, Leadership, Mental Clarity	Shame, Low Self-Esteem, Power Issues, Anger
Emotions and Intimacy	Joy, Creativity, Adaptability, Sensuality, Pleasure, Sexuality	Guilt, Isolation
Physical Existence	Stability, Vitality, Loyalty, Prosperity, Patience, Success	Fear, Anxiety (deals with survival)

Chapter 1

CROWN CHAKRA

Focus: Connecting to Consciousness

The Crown Chakra Sanskrit name is Dahaswara. The meaning in Eastern spiritual practice is the thousands of petals of the sacred lotus flower, a symbol of divine enlightenment. The metaphor relates the gradual opening of the lotus flower to personal and spiritual growth—a subtle aperture to true enlightenment and self-awareness. This Chakra connects you to the non-physical aspect of our existence and helps you make sense of life on this physical plane (C. Tuttle). This also represents that we are spiritual beings having a human experience. Meditation is the best way to connect to the Crown Chakra. It's about emptying your mind, to receive the downloads from the divine. I have pre-recorded meditations for you to use. Keep a journal next to you to see what comes to you as inspiration. I do this every day; I meditate, and then I journal. It helps me get clear on my priorities for my *big* dream. I will know what the next best step is in my path. The process of this book is identifying your desires and receiving guidance from The Universe, known as cosmic connection.

BALANCED ENERGY: To strengthen this Chakra, we must quiet the mind. We declutter by focusing, tuning into the "gap," the space between thoughts. Meditation can help declutter the mind. Creating art can assist with getting into the "zone".

We need to take care of the mind and give it a space to rest in order to perform well and think clearly. The mandala drawings are a great tool for becoming present with the now.

IMBALANCED ENERGY: Depression, alienation, confusion, boredom, apathy, inability to learn, blocked by earthly attachment, spiritual crisis, disorders such as epilepsy, Alzheimer's, multiple sclerosis, dementia, Parkinson's disease, and strokes. A person who is imbalanced will lack purpose in their life.

PHYSICAL BODY: GLANDS: Pituitary, other body parts: cerebral cortex, central nervous system.

FUNCTION IN YOUR LIFE: Understanding creating bliss. Crown Chakra is involved with cosmic energy and consciousness.

ELEMENT: Thought

SYMBOLS: Thousandfold petals of lotus; color is violet to white; planet, Uranus; metal, gold, amethyst, diamond.

COLOR FREQUENCY: purple, gold, and white.

AFFIRMATIONS:

I am intelligent and aware.
I have endless, great ideas.
I am one with everything.

Strengthening Techniques for the Crown Chakra:

1. Wear the color violet.

2. Purple is associated with higher power, spirituality, compassion, sensitivity, and mystery. It relates to the Crown Chakra.

3. Carry the stones: Tourmaline, amethyst, Herkimer diamond, or clear quartz.

4. Affirmation: I am intelligent and aware. I have endless, great ideas. I am one with everything.

5. Practice gratitude every day. Make a list of at least five things you are grateful for in your life. Actively look for things to be grateful for throughout your day. Write them down nightly in a journal.

6. Massage your head daily.

7. Meditate outside. Chakra Activation Meditation (see each Chakra light up)

8. Essential Oils: Lavender, Frankincense, Rosewood.

9. Foods: Fasting

10. Create art using the exercises below.

Art Exercises for Healing: Crown Chakra

1. CROWN CHAKRA MANDALA

BENEFITS: Increases gratitude, self-love, focuses attention, cosmic connection

RELIEF: Reduces stress and negativity

PREP TIME: 10 minutes

ACTIVITY TIME: 50 minutes

MATERIALS:
- Journal
- Pencil
- Assorted drawing media: Colored pencils, gel pens, or markers (various shades of purple and gold)
- Black-ink pen

ACTIVITY HEADNOTE: Tapping into gratitude is one of the most effective ways to connect with Source energy. Make it a daily practice upon waking up to say, "Thank you for another day." Find reasons for gratitude throughout your day, and end your day with documenting those events. Shifts begin to occur. You will find even more things in life to be grateful for, and your energy within will start to feel lighter.

STEPS:

1. Follow the meditation prompt https://leahguzman.com/resource-guide

2. Start with drawing a circle with the pencil.

3. Around the circle, list things in your life you are grateful for at this time.

4. At the center of your circle, you can draw an OM symbol, symbolizing peace. You can add radiating petals of sacred geometry patterns.

5. Use the colors gold, white, and purple to fill in the mandala.

6. Once the coloring is complete, you can go back and add black ink to emphasize and add details

7. Add the affirmations: *I am intelligent and aware. I have endless, great ideas. I am one with everything.*

Note: If you don't want to create your own mandala design, you can print out a copy available on my site. You can use a digital device to add colors as well.

QUESTIONS FOR REFLECTION: Do you notice an energy shift when you focus on gratitude? Can you start looking for gratitude throughout your day to add to your drawing? Ask yourself, *What do I want from The Universe? Be specific. What does The Universe want from me? What do I want to co-create with The Universe?*

Crown Chakra Mandala

Crown Chakra Painting

2. CROWN SYMBOL PAINTING

BENEFITS: Increases self-awareness, peace, and fulfillment

RELIEF: Decreases stress

PREP TIME: 10 minutes

ACTIVITY TIME: 50 minutes

MATERIALS:
- Small canvas (4" x 4" or 6" x 6")
- Lotus Flower image from the internet
- Pencil
- Acrylic Paint (white, gold, shades of purple, green)
- Brushes
- Water container
- Paper towel
- Black ink

ACTIVITY HEADNOTE: The Lotus flower is symbolic of enlightenment. Enlightenment is a deep space within you in which to experience peace, bliss, and contentment. Lotuses represent that you have everything within you that you need. Lotuses grow from dark, muddy waters, opening up to pristine, clean color. It's a metaphor of the intention of this book: We go through darkness and experience contrast in life. We embrace all the feelings, unfold like the lotus, and step into our authenticity. You can use however many petals you desire for this painting.

STEPS:

1. Block in the color purple on the outside of the circle.

2. Choose an image from the Internet of a lotus or sacred geometry symbol that you desire.

3. Sketch out the design on the canvas.

4. Use the white and gold to block in the colors of the design

5. Once dry, add black ink to define design and add an affirmation.

NOTE: You can use the circle as a starting point, or fill up your canvas with your design.

QUESTIONS FOR REFLECTION: Where in life do you feel you see contrast or resistance? How can you see the beauty unfold (lesson in the darkness) like the lotus?

3. LIFE WHEEL

BENEFITS: Increases self-awareness, clarity with direction, focus.

RELIEF: Supports identifying areas of life that are imbalanced.

PREP TIME: 10 minutes

ACTIVITY TIME: 50 minutes

MATERIALS:
- Journal
- Assorted drawing materials (colored pencils, gel pen, or markers)

ACTIVITY HEADNOTE: Take inventory of where you're at now. It's important to identify what you want and where you are at the moment in reaching your goals. The Life Wheel gives you a measuring tool to assess where you are at the moment. Give each piece of your pie a number, so that you can measure where you are now. If you start with a 1, this is just an idea. You have room for growth. There is no judgment with the number, just an opportunity to focus your attention on attaining what you want. I like doing this exercise every other month. I get to see how I've manifested desires, rate myself, and see how the goal manifested. I like to be specific—when I'm working on a project, I name it. This is an adaptation from Esther Hicks, *Focus Wheel*.

- Career (projects)
- Finances (saving, investing, spending, giving)
- Travel
- Spirituality
- Self-care (meditation, art making, journaling, therapy, massages, baths, journaling)
- Relationships (partner, friends, children, business)
- Health (weight, well-being, food, exercise)
- Home (declutter, reorganize, remodel, move the energy)

STEPS:

1. Draw a circle

2. Divide it like a pizza to make eight categories. List category on the edge of the pie slice (refer to image)

3. Write the number you rate yourself of where you are at the moment

4. Color in each category according to your number rating

5. When you check back with yourself a month later, use a different color to see your progress.

NOTE: Keep this in your agenda or journal because you will reflect on it at a later date.

QUESTIONS FOR REFLECTION: Is your wheel imbalanced? What area of your life needs the most attention? Are you willing to get support to help you?

Art Exercises for Manifesting: Crown Chakra

1. LETTER TO THE UNIVERSE

BENEFITS: Increases self-awareness, emotional resilience, identifies strengths.

RELIEF: Clarity on your desire, attuning your energy.

PREP TIME: 10 minutes

ACTIVITY TIME: 50 minutes

MATERIALS:
- Journal
- Pen

ACTIVITY HEADNOTE: The Letter to the Universe is an opportunity to prioritize what you desire. You'll want to get very specific with your desires. Allow yourself to dream big. Practice the visualization exercise to really see the big picture. As you write out your letter, write it in present tense. Here is a list of phrases to avoid. By including lack of "not enough" phrases will only bring more of it. Replace them with higher-vibrational words.

1. I want (says *I don't have*)

2. I wish (says *I don't have*)

3. I hope (says *I don't have*)

4. I need (says *I lack* and *I don't have*)

5. I hate (expresses ungratefulness)

Use these words instead:

1. I will (expresses guaranteed action)
2. I have (acknowledges it into existence)
3. I am (stamps the truth)
4. I love (expresses gratitude)

STEPS:

1. Write it as if you were addressing a letter: "Dear Universe."
2. Start with what you're grateful for at this moment. "Thank you for . . ."
3. Next, reflect on the lessons you've learned this year . . .
4. Did you have challenges? What have you learned from the challenges?
5. Address what is no longer serving you. Release them (thoughts, habits, people, objects).
6. Then, identify what you would like next. "This coming year . . ."
7. List everything you would like to see happen in your life. "I intend to . . ."
8. Write as if it's happened already. Write in present tense.
9. Expand by adding details. Write it out in paragraphs.
10. Sign it with your name.

NOTE: Deepak Chopra suggests reviewing your intentions daily. Keep it with you. You can put it on your phone or in your daily planner. Here is an example of present tense. For example, "I am establishing self-care practices that support my creative business and mental health. I'm able to consistently create and sell my work. My book is published and well received. The money is in the bank. My family and I are healthy. My remodeled house is so beautiful! My artwork is collected and loved around the world."

In utmost gratitude,

(your name)

Questions for Reflection: How did it feel to declare what you want? Was it challenging to write in present tense—as if your desire is already here? Are you feeling resistance or excitement?

2. CO-CREATING YOUR FUTURE ACCORDION BOARD

BENEFITS: Increases self-awareness.

RELIEF: Offers clarity for direction on your path

PREP TIME: 10 minutes

ACTIVITY TIME: 50 minutes to 1 week

MATERIALS:
- Heavy watercolor paper to create accordion board
- Magazines
- Glue stick
- Scissors
- Tape

ACTIVITY HEADNOTE: Collage boards (aka vision boards) are highly effective tools for incorporating the feeling and specifics of what you really want to appear in your life.

This is another opportunity to see your life in a holistic way through art. I've done this as a yearly ritual for more than fifteen years. It's amazing to look back at past boards and see what has manifested. Being specific calls your desires into reality. This may take a week to complete. Be open to finding your imagery throughout your day from various sources (Internet, magazines, out shopping, perusing your emails or social media). You can use both sides of the accordion board to address the different areas of your life. Feel free to do this project digitally as well.

- Relationships
- Projects
- Personal Development
- Career
- Finances
- Travel
- Spirituality
- Self-care
- Health

STEPS:

1. Use large paper and fold into four parts, creating eight sections (an accordion). This also can be adapted for your journal.

2. Choose a word for this year.

3. You can leave breathing space.

4. Play with overlapping.

5. Draw in items you can't find.

6. Print out images from Internet.

7. Add paint to the background.

8. Stay in the feeling of gratitude.

9. Imagine that it's already here.

10. Stretch your imagination.

NOTE: Even if you don't know exactly what you want, stay with the feeling. For example, I know I want to travel with my family for a vacation, yet I'm not sure where. I was attracted to green, lush spaces and paths. It was a feeling of nature and peace. I let the art speak to me about what I would like to experience.

QUESTIONS FOR REFLECTION: Place it in your constant awareness (put it up on the wall so your subconscious mind imprints it). Remember the phrase "This or something better" (what The Universe delivers is always for the greater good of your soul). You don't need to explain yourself to others, because it's no one's business. You are worthy of your dreams, goals, and wishes. Take a photo of your art. Place the photo as wallpaper on your phone, computer, or the cover of your agenda. This process activates your awareness. Trust in The Universe, and believe that all is working out for you.

3. IDEAL SELF AVATAR

BENEFITS: Increases self-awareness, emotional resilience, identifies strengths, uses imagination.

RELIEF: Offers clarity for your direction and where you need to focus your attention.

PREP TIME: 10 minutes

ACTIVITY TIME: 50 minutes

MATERIALS:
- Journal
- Assorted drawing materials (pencil, markers, colored pencils)

ACTIVITY HEADNOTE: Create an avatar of your ideal self. Place your avatar as if you have manifested your desire already. You just had the best year of your life. What happened during this year—what did it look like? Who were you with? What types of relationships do you have? What kind of work are you doing? How much money is in your bank account? Write out your manifestation as if it's already happened. An *avatar* in Sanskrit is a God who can create a world (or universe) and then materialize inside of it. When you consciously create the world you prefer, you are acting as a god or goddess in your Universe. (Anodea Judith) We are intentional, deliberate creators as we step into our ideal self.

STEPS:

1. Use your journal.

2. Draw yourself with a pencil in this image of the best year of your life.

3. Add details to your environment.

4. Pick a color that represents the feeling you have at the time of this manifestation.

5. What is the color of the energy you are vibrating?

6. Color in the avatar and its environment.

NOTE: This is a powerful exercise to use in your daily meditations to visualize yourself living in your ideal reality.

QUESTIONS FOR REFLECTION: What color is your joy? What do you want to show up in your life six months from now? What do you want to show up in your life one year from now? What would you like to see five years from now? Be clear, and put your words in present tense as you reflect. Who do you need to be to bring this to your life? What are some of the characteristics or strengths that you possess in this time? How can you step into this ideal self now?

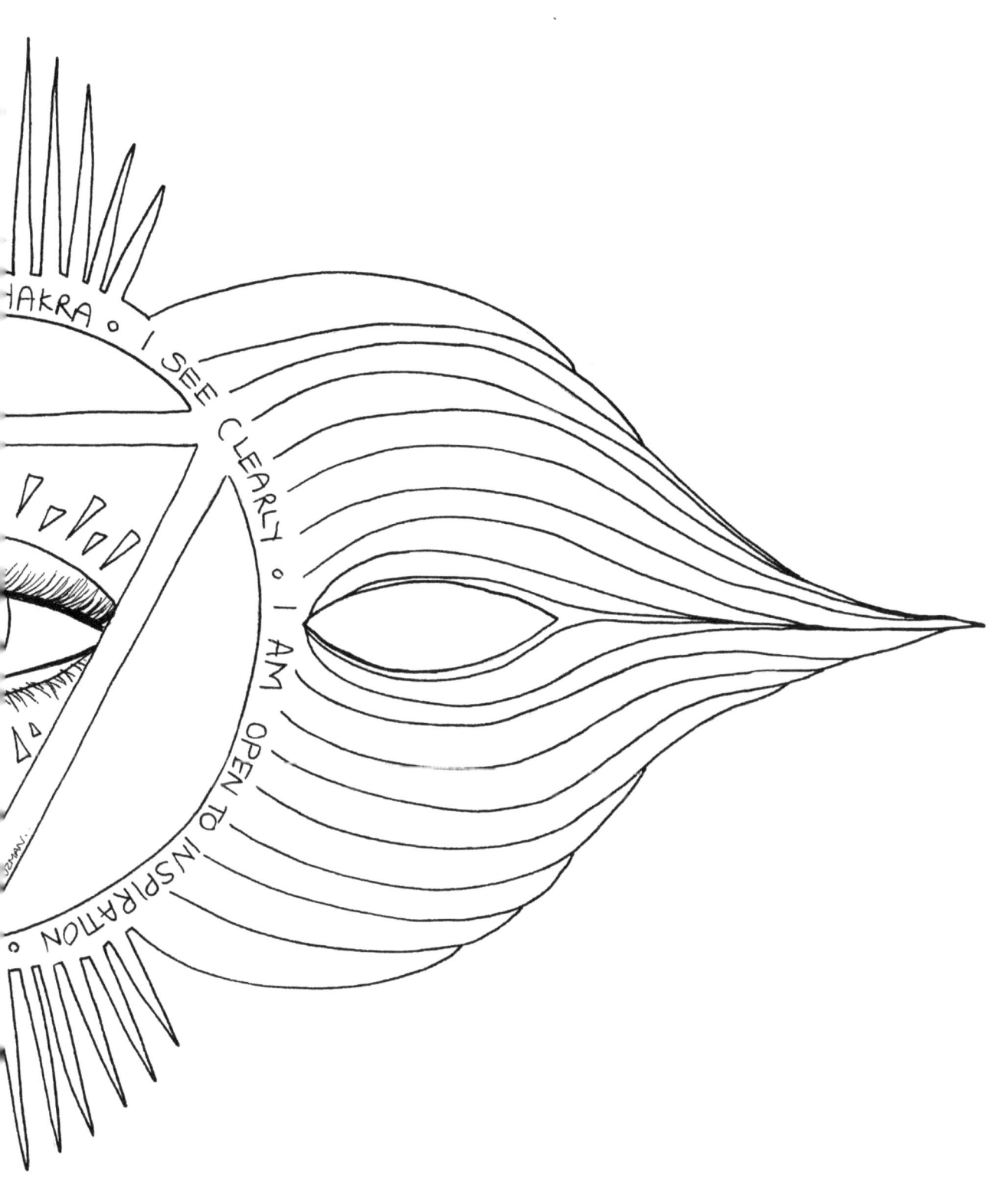

Chapter 2

THIRD-EYE CHAKRA

Focus: Listen to Your Intuition

The Third Eye is located in the center of the forehead. The Sanskrit word is *Anja*. The Third Eye sees beyond the physical world, bringing us added insight and understanding from our higher self. Seeing really does not have to do with our eyes but with our minds. Our desires are guiding forces for envisioning our future. We are here to activate our imagination and dream bigger. The Third-Eye Chakra is all about listening to your intuition, dreaming big, and following the signs along the way. As you become more open to receiving guidance, the signs you receive from The Universe show up more in your life. Synchronicity happens all the time when we tune into these signs. They may show up as numbers, people, or even a chosen symbol (such as a rainbow, bird, or butterfly). The rainbow is one of my signs. When I see one, I feel like The Universe is winking at me and letting me know I'm on the right path.

The challenge of this Chakra is listening to your intuition even when your mind tells you otherwise. The mind is a collection of your memories and experiences—however, it can be limiting. Your intuition is connected to a higher source and can see the big picture. The Third-Eye Chakra connects you to intuition, and it is important to have faith in listening to it. Ultimately, you know what is right for you. Inner vision has much power. Intellect knows only your story, the known. The intellect can be limited by false beliefs, too. The Crown Chakra asks you to focus your intention, and the Third-Eye Chakra asks you to start seeing those images in your mind more clearly.

BALANCED ENERGY: Balanced energy will show up as intuition. Seeing patterns in numbers and symbols from The Universe will occur throughout the day.

IMBALANCED ENERGY/MALFUNCTION: Blindness, headaches, nightmares, eyestrain, blurred vision. The Chakra is blocked by the illusion of separation, that we are divided. Everything is connected.

If the Chakra is spinning too fast, you may experience an overload of visions. You may feel confused about your direction, even overwhelmed.

If it is spinning too slowly, you may have difficulty seeing your vision.

PHYSICAL BODY: GLANDS: pineal. Body parts: eyes. The pineal gland is also known as the "seat of the soul." It acts like a light meter for the body, translating variations in light to hormonal messages related to the body through the autonomic nervous system.

FUNCTION IN YOUR LIFE: Seeing, intuition.

ELEMENT: Light

SYMBOLS: owl, two white petals around a circle, golden triangle pointing downward, crescent moon, Jupiter, Neptune, eyes; color: indigo

COLOR FREQUENCY: Indigo Blue

AFFIRMATIONS:

I am intuitive and follow my inner guidance.
I avidly follow my dreams.
I always see the big picture.

Uncovering your blocks (limiting beliefs)

I love creating my visions through art and visualization. Seeing how I want the big picture to look helps me visualize the details and get into the feeling. However, The Universe

may have something else in store for me. How you deal with the unseen detours on the path can affect your outcome. Doubts can block the manifesting process. Experiencing low-vibration energy can block this process, too. It's important to identify the feeling and be honest with yourself when you become disappointed or things aren't going the way you planned. When this happens, I like to remind myself that The Universe has something even better for me. When something is not on a certain timeline, trust more. I do have a technique in the exercises below that will assist you with identifying your limiting beliefs. Jen Mazer will also discuss this process of dealing with limiting beliefs in her interview.

Interview with Jen Mazer:

Jen Mazer is a transformational speaker and coach. She teaches people how to manifest their biggest dreams while making an impact on the world. She is known for her signature Manifestation Masters program and private success coaching. She has written a book, *Manifesting Made Easy*, and created the game *Sparked* to ignite inspiration and joy.

www.queenofmanifestation.com

LEAH: What is your philosophy about manifesting?

JEN: My background is as an artist, so ever since I was little, I was making art. I was lucky to have really nurturing parents who provided materials for me and took me to art classes. Having that background was really helpful with manifesting. Your imagination is how you tune in, and, so, we've all realized this in different ways as artists. With Divine Inspiration, you get a download, an idea, and you know that that's what you want to create. You're also just in the flow, in the moment, making whatever your craft is, and it feels really natural. You're open, and you're just receiving. You're a channel, and, so, we're all really the arms of The Universe. If we think about us as spiritual beings, whatever your beliefs are, we're all here in this lifetime to create on a physical level.

We're all manifesting, whether we realize it or not. It's just about consciously and intentionally manifesting what you want. When you imagine what you want for your life, you're not just imagining—you're intuiting. When you first have an idea for whatever it is that you want in your life, it's not just you having this crazy idea. You have to actually believe that it's going to happen. Here are some questions to ask yourself: *What is it that I really want? How will I feel when I have that thing that I want?*

Even though I don't yet have the thing I want, I can still feel the way I want to feel now. By feeling that way, then I'm bringing more things into my life that attract that feeling. I might want to buy my dream home, but I haven't bought it yet. I'm going to feel abundant right now. I'm going to feel spacious. I'm going to feel secure. What are things that I can do that will allow me to feel abundant, spacious, and secure right now? I'm acting as if I already am abundant, spacious, and secure. The same thing goes for the actual dream. For example, if I'm going to buy a house, how would that interact with my money? It's going to take inspired action to meet the mortgage lender, even though I don't think I'm ready yet. I'm going to go and get approved for a loan and do it anyway. Just learning about the process and understanding your own finances and doing the steps puts your dream into motion.

QUESTION FROM CREATIVE SOUL SOCIETY MEMBER: I am in the beginning of restarting a business—that is my dream. I'm a healer, I'm an artist, and I'm a visionary. I'm trying to get clarity around what that looks like. How do I combine all my passions and my elements and put that together in an offering? I'm not currently working. I've been on disability for the past year. I've had this gift of a year to really step into my passions, such as reconnecting with my art.

JEN: You can use a personal story. You were just on disability because of how you healed yourself—that's so powerful. We tend to tell lies to ourselves about being confused, when we're really *not* confused. It's really just kind of owning your story and taking that action. For example, "I was on disability leave for a year." I can use that to my advantage because I helped heal myself and then turned this into an offering. By taking action, it's not *getting rid* of fear, because you don't do that. You can't rid yourself of fear. You're just moving it by taking some sort of action. So, maybe, it's sharing a little bit about your story.

I remember this one friend who was a musician, and I was making her website. She had no press yet. She was just starting out, but we made a professional page for her website. I was like, "Let's put a press page up, because then the press will come." And that's exactly what happened. That's how manifesting works.

QUESTION FROM CREATIVE SOUL SOCIETY MEMBER: I'm not sure what to manifest? I don't know which direction to go in?

JEN: It's a common question. So, here's the thing: You can never make a wrong decision. You're never stuck in any situation. So, if we think about quantum physics, the only constant is change. Let's take a moment to look at our physical body. I like to look at my hand as an example. If you zoom into your hand with a microscope, you would see that what looks like solid skin is actually all sorts of molecules, neutrons, and electrons—and everything's in motion. They're all spinning around each other all the time, and that's the same thing in terms of the supposed "separation" between us and this whole technology. We're all connected. It's all in motion. There's motion inside of our bodies. Our bodies on the inside are a mirror of The Universe. If we were to look at The Universe and the planets and solar system, that's what we look like inside our bodies. That's the expansive view. So, we're *connected*. And we're not just *connected* to The Universe—we *are* The Universe. The Universe is inside of us. All the creation power lives inside of you.

We're all natural creators, especially as women. We already have what we need. The eggs are our dreams living inside of us. That's number one. If we think about the Earth, the Earth is rotating on its axis, and it's revolving around the sun at the same time. If we think about vibration, it's common to talk about being in a *high vibe. The high vibe attracts your tribe.* It's all true. People are talking about this because it's that motion piece. We want to feel the movement in our own lives, that *high vibration*. In high vibrations, we don't have stuck energy in our own body. If we've got stuck energy or limiting beliefs, we're going to feel stuck. There's no movement. So, the question is, *How can we get unstuck?*

Number one, you can move your body. That's helpful, but you can take any action. The action will move you forward in your own life and vibration. If you think about a rainbow, every color is connected. It's not just that there's red, orange, yellow, green, blue, purple. There are actually *millions* of colors in that spectrum, because one leads to the next. There's no separation in color, and it's the same with us and The Universe. It's the same thing with us and our dreams—it's all connected.

When you realize that you can have *all* of your dreams, the question becomes, *What do I want to prioritize first? Which dream is going to move my life further the fastest and have a ripple effect on everything else in my life?* Start with that one thing—and prioritize it. The trick is that most of us don't ever get to that priority because we're too busy in the day-to-day survival mode. We put that big dream on the back burner. We think, "Oh, one day when I figure it all out or when I've got enough time or money." So, just put it on the front burner. Make it number one on your to-do list. As scary as that is, when you do that and take action on that small action, it's something that's going to move it forward every day. Then it's going to happen *automatically*. In a month, you'll be, like, "I can't believe it! Whoa—what a difference!"

LEAH: Can you talk about a way to clear our limiting beliefs?

JEN: The thing is, we *all* have limiting beliefs. The secret is to just not be afraid of them—because they're normal—for everybody. I like to think of it as an onion. We've cleared maybe the first few layers of that onion, and we're, like, "Oh, I've done the work on myself, and then, all of a sudden, you *go big*, and you take action on a new dream—and something else pops up. "Oh, there's just another layer." If we were to start the manifestation process with limiting beliefs, we would never take action. We would never go anywhere because we'd be stuck in our story.

You don't want to start the process there. You always want to start the process with getting clear on what you want and letting yourself imagine—because the first step in manifesting is allowing yourself to *imagine*. Most people block themselves in the very beginning. They don't even open up and allow themselves to dream bigger. They're just dreaming based on their current circumstances. *Dreaming big* means taking yourself out of your current circumstances. If you could *do anything, be anything*, what would you do? Where would you be? Who would you be hanging out with? What would you be creating?

Every obstacle is an opportunity. The opportunity may be clearing something that you've been holding on to or to get yourself into better alignment. We can clear that and keep going and keep going. In terms of manifesting, there's no such thing as "trying." Watch the way you talk about what you're doing. "I'm going to try this dating site" or "I'm going to try to make this piece of art" or whatever it is. Speaking in terms of "I'm going to try to launch this course" is counter-productive. *You're either doing it or you're not.* When you're doing it, you expect that it's going to happen. That's what makes a powerful manifestation. We expect that it's all going to work out. Manifesting happens in the present tense. You shouldn't say, "I will do that" because if we say,

"I will," then it's always going to stay out in the future. It needs to be in the present tense. If you say, "I want," that means that you're in a place of *lacking*. For example, if you really can't afford it, and you're looking in your bank account. The negative feels bad—it reinforces the belief that you don't want to have. So instead, you should say, "How can I?" Open it up to a question. "I can't" becomes a new phrase—"How can I? I'm open for The Universe to show me a sign, or my own intuition will show me. I'm going to journal to find a way."

The language that you use is really important. When you say, "I can't," it puts you in a victim role instead of a power position. When you change "I have to" to "I get to," it puts you in a place of power.

This goes back to quantum physics, which is the Law of Attraction. We live in a participatory Universe. In quantum physics, thoughts right now affect the outcome of our lives, so we change our thoughts in this moment so that we can change the outcome. We're all connected to the Universal Field, which is that vibration. *I'm not a victim of my circumstance. I can always choose again, and choose again, and choose again.* It's not just about being a participant and being in charge. Another way to participate is to be in gratitude. The more you're in gratitude, the more you're grateful for what you already have, and the more comes in to be grateful for. We can ask ourselves, "Am I practicing gratitude regularly?" Women, in particular, feel guilty for what we're *not* doing, like the things on our to-do list we didn't complete. We replay them in our mind over and over again instead of focusing on how awesome we are and what we *did* get done. The happier you are, the more the opportunities that come in.

LEAH: Can we talk about money and how it relates to our services and art?

JEN: As an artist, the value is not you. Most of us attach value to ourselves without realizing that's what we're doing. When I offer a program—whether it's private coaching or an online program—it's about transformational work, so it's the value of the transformation. The value of the joy that someone is going to get from this piece. If someone rejects it, they are not rejecting you—they just don't resonate with the work.

Set intentions in your journal, like an affirmation but in paragraph form. It's not just short sentences. For example, I have great clients and describe them in all the details. Nobody has to see this but you. People love my work—they flock to it. I have an art show that sells out on the first day on opening night. This amazing collector purchases my art, and all my pieces sell for more than $5,000. I always like to use the words "more than" in my money statements because then I'm not limiting it to being only this amount. I make *more than* this amount; I sell this piece for *more than* this amount. It sells easily and quickly, and the perfect buyer who gets it loves my work. She takes me out to dinner; we become best friends and go on trips together. Talk about you knowing those people in detail—like what you love about them and what they love about you. You always want to be reciprocal when writing your intentions. I notice people are one-sided in how they're talking about the relationship: "I'm so in love with my partner, and I love doing this and this," or "You know he loves me" but let's be reciprocal. "I love this, and he loves this, and we love doing this together." I love my clients, and my clients love me. They respect me; they always pay on time, and they pay me more than what I ask for. Let's play as creators, as artists, as manifesters, so it's playful energy. This is fun—it's a game.

CREATIVE SOUL SOCIETY MEMBER QUESTION: I have a question about timeline and manifesting. How do you balance personal expectation that something's going to show up in a certain amount of time?

JEN: It's good to set an intention for when you want things to come in. I like to actually put dates in my calendar. It's not just about writing an affirmation by this future date. What I do to prepare myself for that event is to take some new action. With all manifesting, there is a gestational period, as in a garden. We're planting seeds first; then seeds grow down in the dirt. We can't see them when they are growing roots. They are taking hold, creating a solid foundation. This unseen activity is necessary in order for them to sprout up beneath you, above the surface, and then grow and blossom. Wherever we are in our process of manifesting, it might look like dirt, but it's trusting that stuff is happening, even though we can't see it. Continue to water and nurture our dreams in the garden until we see the physical manifestation. It's trusting in divine timing. If it didn't happen, there must be some reason why it's not happening right now. Even though it may be disappointing, I know something even better is on the way.

Meditation: IDEAL SELF GUIDED VISUALIZATION
https://leahguzman.com/resource-guide

Try this guided meditation to tune in, listen, and reflect on where you are in your life.

Find a comfortable seat on your couch, chair, or in your favorite place in nature.

Settle into your body by connecting with your breath—slowly inhale through your nose, slowly exhale through your mouth. Notice how your body and mind begin to soften and relax.

Visualize a scene from nature. It may be the ocean, the mountains, the forest, a stream, or even the desert. Now, imagine that your body, breath, emotions, and mind are an extension of nature. Perhaps you see yourself as a tall oak tree, a wave on the ocean, or as simply lying in the grass.

You are about to embark on an inward journey. We are taking the time to imagine:

- the person you would like to be
- the activities you want to do
- the environment you thrive in most
- the lifestyle you want to have when you wake up every day

Let your imagination run wild, and allow yourself to see what you would see, to hear what you would hear, and to feel what you would feel if your dream came true.

Next, think of an area of your life where you feel stuck. It may feel heavy, restricted, and uncomfortable. In what area of your life do you feel this heaviness? Is it your intimate relationship, your career, your health and fitness, or family? Let yourself see where there is an over-accumulation of physical stuff, emotional upset, mental challenges, or spiritual disconnect.

Now go back to reconnect with your ideal self. What could your life look like, feel like, and sound like once you are free from the resistance? What would you be doing then that is different from how you are living now? How would your relationships begin to thrive? How would your energy levels and mental clarity be propelling you toward your goals? Create an internal representation (a visual image, a feeling, or a sound) of how you, your life, and your surroundings could be different.

What qualities would you need to embrace to be the type of person who could be living the life that you desire? Do you need to show up more with your art and gifts? Do you need to listen more attentively without the need to fix things or justify your position? Do you need to cultivate more strength so you can set and maintain boundaries? Do you need to be more honest and find a loving yet direct way to speak your truth? What characteristics would be most beneficial to acquire so that you can begin to take your next steps?

Now, envisioning the traits or characteristics that are empowering you to create change, ask yourself, *What action steps do I need to take to feel inspired and motivated to charge powerfully forward? What emotions, beliefs, or behaviors do I need to let go of so that I can stop being a victim and become the person I am meant to be?* Ask your heart for guidance rather than your intellect, and allow yourself to hear what practice you need to cultivate.

When you are ready, take a few slow, deep breaths, and open your eyes. Take out your journal or notebook, and go ahead and start your art. Pick an exercise that resonates with you from this section.

Strengthening techniques for the Third-Eye Chakra:

1. Essential Oils: Citrus Lemon, Sandalwood

2. Meditate with your vision

3. Wear the dark-blue color. Dark blue is associated with the Third-Eye Chakra. It relates to listening to your intuition and following the signs of The Universe. The color brings the feeling of inner security, trust, and calmness. If the Chakra is imbalanced, you will feel a lack of intuition.

4. Create art related to this Chakra.

Healing Art Exercises: Third-Eye Chakra

1. ALL-SEEING MANDALA

BENEFITS: Increases self-awareness, focus, mindfulness

RELIEF: Reduces stress

PREP TIME: 10 minutes

ACTIVITY TIME: 50 minutes

MATERIALS:
- Journal
- Pencil
- Assorted drawing materials: Colored pencils, markers, gel pens (various shades of blue, gold, and silver)
- Fine-point black pen

ACTIVITY HEADNOTE: This exercise helps get you in the meditative-zone headspace. If you need healing or want guidance from your intuition, it is necessary for you to slow down in order to receive the messages. Practicing mandala drawing gives you this opportunity. You might be questioning yourself from the last healing exercise, "How do I change my mindset?" It's reframing how you look at the situation. By including affirmations in your intentional art-making, it will reprogram your subconscious mind. For a long time, I didn't see my own value in the artwork I created. I had to reprogram by creating affirmations that I would see every day that stated, "My artwork is powerful, healing, and important in the world."

STEPS:

1. Close your eyes, and set your intention for this piece.

2. Ask your higher self a question for guidance.

3. In your journal, draw a circle with your pencil.

4. Write out your intention in your journal.

5. Draw the "OM" symbol in the center.

6. Add an upside-down triangle and two lotus petals to create your "All-Seeing Eye."

7. Once sketched, add colors of the Third Eye, various dark blues.

8. Use the black-ink pen to outline and emphasize the drawing.

9. Add an affirmation and your gratitude: *I am intuitive and follow my inner guidance. I avidly follow my dreams. I always see the big picture. My work is important in the world.*

10. Title your piece on the back.

NOTE: You can also use paint as alternative media if you prefer.

QUESTIONS FOR REFLECTION: What message came to you while you were creating? By giving yourself space, you will receive the message from your higher self.

2. THIRD-EYE CHAKRA PAINTING WITH SYMBOLS

BENEFITS: Connecting to Your Intuition

RELIEF: Releasing fears, doubts

PREP TIME: 10 minutes

ACTIVITY TIME: 50 minutes

MATERIALS:
- Small canvas (4" x 4" or 6" x 6")
- Pencil
- Acrylic paint (white, indigo-blue, silver, or gold)
- Brushes
- Paint palette
- Water container
- Paper towel
- Black Pen (fine-point marker)
- Printout of an owl, Om symbol, or eye online

ACTIVITY HEADNOTE: The intention of this exercise is to use the color, symbols, and message of the Third-Eye Chakra to tap into your intuition. Using the color of this Chakra, indigo-blue, is a way to help balance this Chakra. We want our intuition to be the guiding force in our lives. When we can *feel* our way intuitively to the next best step, life gets easier and in the flow. The owl is symbolic of connecting to the spirit world and tapping into insight. Give yourself time and space to receive the downloads from spirit. You can practice the associated meditation. The owl is a powerful totem animal that brings truth and protection.

STEPS:

1. Draw a large circle on the canvas.

2. Block in outside of the circle with the color indigo.

3. Look up an image of an owl or eye online. Choose one to paint.

4. By looking at the image, draw your own version on the canvas with pencil.

5. Add paint to fill in space.

6. Next, once the paint is dry, use the black-ink pen to fill in the eyes, beak, and outline.

7. Place your canvas on the wall to view daily.

NOTE: If you need support drawing your owl, you can print a small version of one, and simply paste in your journal. Fill the owl in with paint. You can also exchange the "owl" and draw the "eye" for your symbol. Also, you can use your whole canvas for the subject if you prefer not to use the circle.

QUESTIONS FOR REFLECTION: In which area of your life do you wish to seek guidance? What areas of your life do you feel that you need to surrender? You can literally sit on your knees and let The Universe know that you are surrendering. Ask for guidance.

3. UNCOVERING YOUR BLOCK

BENEFITS: Increases self-awareness, emotional resilience, identifies strengths

RELIEF: Anxiety, Depression, PTSD

PREP TIME: 10 minutes

ACTIVITY TIME: 50 minutes

MATERIALS:
- Journal
- Assorted Drawing Materials (markers, colored pencils)

ACTIVITY HEADNOTE: It is natural to feel fear or notice a voice of doubt come up related to our desires. Usually it's our Ego trying to protect us. Becoming aware of it, really feeling it, and exploring its purpose for being there will release it. For example, many of my clients want to sell more art and offer workshops. Yet, they have a fear about pricing their work or not being understood by people. A fear of judgment stops them from showing up to their soul's desire. This is an opportunity to look at what is stopping you in order to have a relationship with your Ego. As the little voice comes up, you can speak to it, *"I know who you are (Ego)."* This little voice comes up when I launch a new series of art. It will say, "No one will care about your work." I respond, "It's okay, because I know my work is important in this world, and I choose to share it without attachment to a response." The affirmation-manifesting exercise is a great tool to use as support in reframing your words to yourself. Use the Avatar as a way to separate yourself from the actual fear. You can even speak to the Avatar using the self-reflection questions. This block may be your Ego, a limiting belief, or shadow side of yourself. Pick which one you think is stopping you.

STEPS:

1. Identify three things that are stopping you from manifesting your desire. Write them down in your journal.

2. Next, write out the story of why you can't have what you want.

3. Choose a color to represent your fear or block.

4. Create an Avatar of your block or limiting belief. It can be a human figure or even a monster.

5. Draw the figure, using shapes.

6. Draw the Avatar in an environment.

7. Give it a name.

8. Fill the page with color.

NOTE: You can also use photography to represent the "Shadow" self. You can take a picture of an image (or you) with a shadow.

QUESTIONS FOR REFLECTION: Are you afraid people will judge you? Do you feel that what you offer isn't important? Do you think you don't have time to do it? Do you think you can't afford it? All of these are very common blocks. What would you do if you weren't afraid? It's really about changing your mindset and knowing that your desire has to be bigger than your fear. To take this exercise to the next step, create affirmations that are the opposite of your limiting beliefs.

Manifesting Art Exercises: Third-Eye Chakra

1. MY IDEAL DAY

BENEFITS: Increases self-awareness, emotional resilience, identifies strengths

RELIEF: Supports your imagination, listening to your intuition, and goal setting

PREP TIME: 10 minutes

ACTIVITY TIME: 50 minutes

MATERIALS:
- Journal
- Assorted pens
- Colored pencil

ACTIVITY HEADNOTE: Draw out your ideal day. From the moment you wake up in the morning, you get to choose how you spend your time and who you want to spend it with. Dream big. Live the life you love. Level up every area of your life: finances, creative projects, relationships, business, health, spiritual practice, travel. People who get into the habit of dreaming big allow themselves the opportunity to accomplish their goals more often than those who do not. Daydreaming has always been one of my favorite activities—thinking about my ideal days. If you had a magic wand and it could make your desire come to life, what would it look like?

STEPS:

1. Take the time to visualize your *big* desire

2. Close your eyes and imagine waking up. Your manifestation is happening.

3. Draw out the details of your ideal day in your journal.

4. Add details and color.

NOTE: If there are parts of the day that you can't visualize, then it could represent that it's not meant for you right now. For example, if you were wanting to manifest a lover, yet you couldn't "see" what this person would look like in your day, then it could represent you may need to focus your attention on self-love for the time being. Include self-love rituals throughout your day.

QUESTIONS FOR REFLECTION: How does it feel to see the details of your everyday life? What is something that you can do today that will take you closer to the next step? Are you desiring a new home? Then go and visit an open house that has your specific preferences. Start thinking of ways to act as if it's already here.

2. ASK FOR SIGNS OF ALIGNMENT/REVEALING A MESSAGE FROM SPIRIT GUIDES

BENEFITS: Increases self-awareness, emotional resilience, identifies strengths

RELIEF: Supports you on your path

PREP TIME: 10 minutes

ACTIVITY TIME: 50 minutes

MATERIALS:
- Journal
- Assorted drawing materials (gel pens, colored pencils, markers)

ACTIVITY HEADNOTE: In this exercise, you are co-creating with The Universe and asking for a sign to let you know that your request is being processed. Your request can be a number sequence, a bird, feather, special object, or anything that represents to you a connection to Divine Source. For me, I feel very connected when I see a rainbow. I do live in a tropical paradise, where rainbows are frequent. Yet, the rainbow is a sign of my connection and can come in many different ways. For example, I asked The Universe for a sign of following my path of expansion and letting people know more about my processes. I asked for a rainbow to let me know I'm going on the right path.

During my art therapy session with a young child, he was cleaning his paint palette. He exclaimed, "Come here, Mrs. Guzman. Come look at my rainbow!" At that moment, I lit up! Thank you, Universe, for my sign today.

If you need a sign, you can ask for one. You can ask for a specific sign. If you are looking for an answer to something, ask The Universe to show you the way. Co-creation is being open to possibilities and opportunities. This is about feeling your way to the next best step.

STEPS:

1. Choose your sign (for example, a number sequence, feather, bird, word).

2. Use your assorted drawing materials to write out your question.

3. Draw your sign.

4. Be open to receiving a message.

NOTE: What happens if you don't receive your sign? Gabby Bernstein is one of my favorite spiritual teachers and discusses how, when you don't see a sign, *that's* a sign, too! It's a message that you may need to change course. Remember, your desire is the best scenario for everyone. How will your desire affect the people and loved ones around you?

QUESTIONS FOR REFLECTION: What signs did you receive? You can look up the meaning of the sign online as well. For example, if you chose a feather as your sign, what type of feather is it? Look up the bird symbolism, because it has a message for you. The Universe is always speaking to us.

3. MANIFESTING BOX

BENEFITS: Increases faith in divine timing

RELIEF: Surrendering your desires to The Universe

PREP TIME: 10 minutes

ACTIVITY TIME: 50 minutes

MATERIALS:
- Box (tissue, wooden cigar box, jewelry box)
- Acrylic paint
- Journal
- Water container
- Paint palette
- Brushes
- Paper towel

ACTIVITY HEADNOTE: This exercise gives you the opportunity to take your visualizations and release your desires. You are always being supported. It's important to ask for guidance. It's also important to trust. This exercise was adapted by Esther Hicks. The box symbolically represents love (Universe) holding your desire and taking care of it for you. I like to start with doing a gridding technique that will open your heart space. Each activity you think of to place in your grid can change your vibration to a love frequency. I love how you can choose the colors that match the vibration for you.

STEPS:

1. Practice gridding exercise from Abraham Hicks.

2. Draw a grid with nine squares in your journal.

3. For each space in the grid, think of an activity that you love; add the emotion associated with the activity. For example, I love roller skating because it gives me freedom. Write "Freedom" in one box. I love waking up early to meditate and write in my journal. It makes my mornings feel relaxed. Write "Relaxed" in the grid.

4. Do this until all nine boxes are filled.

5. Choose a color to match each emotion from the grid.

6. Paint the outside of the box with the colors chosen.

7. Next, pick something you want to manifest, and write it on a card or paper.

8. Place inside the box.

9. Whenever a desire comes up, write it down, and place it inside the box.

NOTE: Can you see how the box is holding the vibration of love?

QUESTIONS FOR REFLECTION: How does it feel to release your desires? Is it scary? Do you have any doubts? Resistance? If any of these emotions come up, you can release them by writing them down on a small piece of paper and burning them. Be sure to have water near to extinguish them.

Trust the Process

Where in your life do you need to surrender to the process? You might have a great art idea or big business dream? Ask for the sign and trust the process. Let the Universe guide you even if you can't see the entire path.

Chapter 3

THROAT CHAKRA

Focus: Communication and Creativity

The location of the 5th Chakra is in the throat. In Sanskrit the throat Chakra is *Vishuddha*, the center of expression and communication. Communication is vital for our existence, starting with our cells relating to people in the world. Communication is the process of transmitting and receiving information. We are able to communicate through our voice, symbols, written text, and art.

Communication is the art of connection. Communication is the act of bringing an abstract thought into a tangible, manifested idea. The throat Chakra is about communicating and expressing your needs and listening to others. In manifesting our desires, we need to express them to people. As a creative, sharing your work with people, growing your business to expand, planning a trip, or even meeting a lover, we need to claim it! Exclaim it! Speak it into reality. We will be creating mantras and affirmations to use as daily reminders. In order to manifest, you have to believe what you want can really happen. Daily reading of your desire will plant it into your subconscious mind. Train your brain to believe. Even the words we tell ourselves have so much power. When our throat Chakra is blocked, we will often feel that we are not being heard. If your throat Chakra is open, you become skillful in expressing your needs. You trust that The Universe will bring you the right speech and handle the details when expressing yourself.

Balanced Energy

When the throat Chakra is open and balanced, you will find the right words in any situation. You will be honest and express your true self. You will feel confident in speaking up for yourself. Others will hear you and receive what you have to say.

IMBALANCED ENERGY/MALFUNCTION: Sore throat, stiff neck, colds, thyroid problems, hearing problems, blocked by lies. We need to be careful of the words we tell ourselves. Our words have power. If your throat Chakra is weak, you may second-guess yourself or may not find the words to express yourself.

If your throat Chakra is spinning too fast, you may speak quickly, talk over people, or not take the time to listen to other people's needs. If your throat Chakra is spinning too slow, you may not speak up for yourself, have negative self-talk, difficulty with expression, lack creativity, and criticize yourself or others

Throat-Chakra imbalances may stem from childhood. We learn self-talk from our parents and the words they tell us; this is conditioning. Research shows that self-talk is extremely powerful. When we encounter stress, how we speak to ourselves will either support or break you. To build emotional intelligence, have a healthy relationship with the words you tell yourself. According to Dr. Shpancer, in a post from *Psychology Today*, a way to reframe your self-talk is to speak to yourself in the third person. For example, if you didn't have the best launch of your new art series or online course, is your first response, "I suck!"? Put yourself in the second or third person: "How could Leah do this better next time?" This gives you an opportunity to distance yourself from your own negative reaction. The study concluded that those individuals who used the word "I" when thinking about worrisome issues in their lives had more stress. The individuals who switched their inner dialogue to second or third person had fewer negative emotions.

One of the healing exercises below is a journaling technique of talking to your inner child. It is time to find your voice. You can do this by talking to your inner child. Ask it what it needs. With your non-dominant hand, have the child write you back. Respect your inner child, and listen to what they have to say.

The theme of this Chakra is to "*Open up* to Your *Truth*." We will start with ourselves. Do you have limiting beliefs? Do you tell yourself lies? Do you stop yourself from pursuing your dreams or listening to your heart? Affirmations can be an extremely powerful way to make a change. Affirmations can support rewiring your brain and change your limited beliefs. We will start with ourselves and use the words *I am*.

PHYSICAL COMPONENT: GLANDS: thyroid, parathyroid, other body parts, neck, shoulder, arms, and hands

ELEMENT: Sound

SYMBOLS: bright cerulean-blue color, sixteen-petal lotus, planet Mercury, turquoise, white elephant, bull, lion

COLOR FREQUENCY: Bright Blue

AFFIRMATIONS:

I know my truth, and I share it.
My life is guided by divine synchronicity.
I am guided by my deepest purpose.

MEDITATION: Cosmic Energy meditation
Inspired by Roger Gabriel
https://leahguzman.com/resource-guide

Tap into it. Imagine your higher self hovering above your head. Imagine a tube of light connecting to your higher self through your body. Imagine the light energizing your whole body. Your whole body lights up and is activated by the energy. As you stay in this cosmic field, you feel lighter and brighter. When you're ready, share the energy with those around you. Imagine sharing the light with them.

Interview with Lana Shlafer

Lana Shlafer is a mindset coach, Law of Attraction expert, and author of the best-selling book *Manifest That Miracle*.

Over the past decade, she has empowered thousands of clients and students to manifest what seems out of reach, including buying their dream home, healing from a chronic illness, and meeting their ideal partner.

More than 20,000 people have participated in her Manifesting Challenges. Lana's energetic personality and no-holds-barred coaching has been featured in Forbes, TVOne, and NPR.

Lana studied at UC Berkeley and the Institute of Transpersonal Psychology. She lives in Puerto Rico with her amazing husband and three magical kids.
www.lanashlafer.com

LEAH: I've enjoyed your book, and one of the quotes that sticks out for me is, "Stop, drop, realign, we access the divine!" I was thinking we could start out talking about manifesting and the first steps. Let's break it down.

LANA: I feel that "manifesting" is creating something deliberately. Most people differentiate between "manifesting" and "achieving" by saying that "manifesting" has an element of *support* and *ease* to it—frequently from beyond the physical realm, but not necessarily so. To "make manifest" is to "make happen," so I actually use that term very often, yet it's not what I lead with. It's making it your everyday way of approaching your decisions, your choices, your visions of the future, your goals, so it's something that you actually utilize as a way to live your life—not just a way to get over there. It's an everyday practice of finding those different tools to get there.

LEAH: You use the term "colored good." Can you tell us more about that viewpoint?

LANA: A satisfying, extraordinary life is not chasing manifestations—it's becoming someone who can see the good in any situation and discern the miracle in it. It starts with the assumption that all circumstances are inherently neutral, and whatever you assign to it is what you will derive from it. If you can "color it good," you will be able to derive good even from the most challenging, painful, horrible situation. Even those situations have within them the seeds of a blessing.

LEAH: How do you allow the space to process low-vibration emotions such as grief so that they aren't suppressed?

LANA: By making it overtly clear that all emotions have a purpose. In the teachings of Abraham, Esther and Jerry Hicks started channeling and teaching the Law of Attraction. They discuss an "emotional guidance system," on which they list 22 emotions. The lowest on the guidance scale are powerlessness, fear, and depression. Then you move up to revenge, anger, disappointment, and shame. Then you keep going up and up and up to get neutral and positive emotions. The problem is that people, including me, focused on the scale and treated it as if it were a hierarchy. Yet, I see it more of an emotional keyboard. You have the lower notes and the higher notes. It will not sound great if you jump from the lower notes to the higher notes without playing somewhere in between. So, you acknowledge the notes as valuable (it's annoying when somebody just stays on the high notes), which is called "spiritual bypassing." Authentically, no one can stay on one note; it's not grounded in the rest of human experiences in life.

Now, when you take away the charge of the negative emotions as being bad or unnecessary, you develop the capacity to feel safe. Anything that doesn't go your way creates an opening—you're no longer hostage to things being a certain way, so you can avoid all those emotions. You want to create room to honor the emotion, feel the grief, feel the sadness—*normalize* the emotion. *All* the emotions can be used as fuel for growth and manifesting; whatever is happening could be "colored good." If you honor where you're at, it naturally blossoms to the next emotion. We do desire to feel good—it's a natural human desire. Michael Beckwith's quote is, "It's not my work to make it *happen*—it's my work to make it *welcome*." It's about offering an experience to get comfortable with any emotion to receive the gift in it.

LEAH: What is the coolest manifestation from one of your clients?

LANA: I would say there's a bunch of health miracles. They are amazing because they're quite specific about being sick—and then you're not sick. It's about having a full experience of life even though you have a disability, detriment, or chronic illness. My master coach had Crohn's disease, and we started working together. It was very debilitating. She didn't think she could leave the house for more than an hour a day. She wasn't able to fully function. She would go to work, but she had this fear that she'd have to run to the toilet. It was an extreme case. Now, she has none of the concerns she had before. She is able to teach dance and feel healthy. I had another client who was in litigation with an employer, and, during the course, she was awarded a six-figure settlement. Another client was on the brink of divorce because she had cheated. They had two kids, and she wanted to exit the relationship. She was able to do deep healing work to honor herself. She was then able to do a healing journey with her partner. So, every time I see the entire family on Facebook, it's really rewarding for me. She was able to find her own happiness.

LEAH: How do you teach your children about manifesting?

LANA: You don't—you just lead by example. It's not structured or ritualistic. It's how I approach life—so when there are opportunities, when there are conflicts and challenges, we can learn how to "color it good." Most people must think I'm positive all the time. I want them to see the conflict and contrast; my husband and I want them to see people upset. When we argue, we aren't doing it behind closed doors. We also process it after, so they don't internalize it.

LEAH: Can you tell us about your vulnerability posts? Many artists and art therapists are challenged when it comes to sharing their gifts. Can you tell us more about your intention of being vulnerable on social media?

LANA: It's a consistent way for me to feel into my edges and to own the parts. Right now, my life looks very glamorous. I see an endless ocean out my office window every day. I used to have really thin hair and couldn't grow my hair long. I adopted the mindset of what it would feel like to be more glamorous with long hair. I've never had long hair in my adulthood, and now I have long hair. There have been a few comments that people have made about my life being perfect. Even though I talk about my challenges, I am pretty invincible and empowered. I hit my limits and growth edges, but the truth is that I have an awesome life. I do vulnerability posts so people can see me as a person, as a human. It feels good to feel uncomfortable—it's connecting with people. It's very authentic. You can just show up and be yourself. You can wake up and be upset and be open about it.

My parents were very well-meaning, but, unintentionally, I picked up this idea that, just by my nature and my inability to hold feelings in, I would be hurting people. So, it became important for me to express myself, because it wasn't allowed; it wasn't welcomed. It has developed into my superpower, one to which other people are drawn, and it all stemmed from pain. We create our greatest gains from pain. It feels very full circle.

Strengthening Techniques for the Throat Chakra:

1. Release your denial and the lies you tell yourself. Accept who you are.

2. Wear the color light blue. Bright blue brings the feeling of freedom, self-expression, and trustworthiness. If you're balanced, you will feel expressive and artistic—you can express yourself clearly. If you're imbalanced, you may be speaking too much or not being heard.

3. Speak your desires as present tense. As if they are in your reality now.

4. Carry blue stones: Turquoise, Apatite, Sodalite or Azurite

5. Essential Oils: Frankincense, Blue Chamomile

Healing Art Exercises: Throat Chakra

1. THROAT CHAKRA MANDALA

BENEFITS: Increases self-awareness, emotional resilience, identifies strengths

RELIEF: Anxiety, Depression, PTSD

PREP TIME: 10 minutes

ACTIVITY TIME: 50 minutes

MATERIALS:
- Journal
- Assorted drawing materials
- Black pen

ACTIVITY HEADNOTE: The healing throat Chakra mandala focuses your attention on expressing your needs. Let The Universe know through the writing exercise. Identify areas in your life where you feel that you need to be heard so you can consciously bring awareness and make a change. I've noticed this comes up in my own life when I'm sharing my art and services. My color palette includes bright blue intentionally to help heal and express myself. I also see this in my clients' lives as well, when they want to show up and share their gifts, yet they're scared of being judged. Our Ego likes to keep us small because it's protecting us. It's concerned with what people might think. Your creative practice is a gift to the world. It's an act of self-care. Sharing your art and services will cause ripple effects all around you in a positive way. As you go through these exercises, you will see how the Chakras are connected. Speaking up also relates to your solar plexus Chakra about standing in your power. You can add your desires into the mandala, the bright-blue color, and the affirmations associated with helping to balance the throat Chakra.

STEPS:

1. Start with tracing a circle with a pencil. You can use a bowl, plate, or anything circular to trace a circle.

2. Next, draw out the throat Chakra symbol in the center.

3. Following the circle, write out the affirmations associated with the throat Chakra.

4. Include the empowering affirmations that you created from your limited-belief story.

5. Add a design.

6. Once it's drawn with pencil, go back and trace the pencil with ink.

7. Color in the image with varying shades of bright blue.

8. Post image up to see daily as a reminder to use your voice.

QUESTIONS FOR REFLECTION: What is it that you want? Where do you feel invisible or not heard? Are you scared of being judged? Write an affirmation to include in your mandala that affirms your importance in the world. One of my affirmations that helped me show up to share my art was, "My artwork is powerful, healing, and important in the world."

2. THROAT CHAKRA PAINTING WITH SYMBOLS

BENEFITS: Increases self-awareness and emotional resilience, identifies strengths

RELIEF: Supports healing through associated color frequency

PREP TIME: 10 minutes

ACTIVITY TIME: 50 minutes

MATERIALS:
- Small canvas (4" x 4" or 6" x 6")
- Pencil
- Acrylic paint (white, bright blue, silver, or gold)
- Brushes
- Paint palette
- Water container
- Paper towel
- Black Pen (fine-point marker)

ACTIVITY HEADNOTE: In this painting, you have the opportunity to connect with your voice. Declare what you want to receive and give in life. The symbols have meanings. Choose which one resonates with you. Birds give freedom of expression. The whale sings songs of the soul. Wolves howl the heart's desire. The animal will help you tap into the energies, and you will gain strength, courage, and guidance.

STEPS:

1. Draw a circle.

2. Choose a symbol that resonates with you. Look up the animal symbol (bull, white elephant, wolf, birds, whale). You can also use the element design of sound. Or, you can choose your own symbol that represents your desire to draw.

3. Draw your version on the canvas with pencil inside the circle.

4. Add bright-blue paint on the outside of the circle.

5. Block in colors of your symbol.

6. Once the paint is dry, use black ink to outline and add affirmations.

QUESTIONS FOR REFLECTION: Where are you "playing small" in your life? Are you scared that people will judge you? Do you fear rejection? How can you take on these strengths of the animal you chose in your day?

3. INNER-CHILD CONNECTION

BENEFITS: Increases self-awareness and emotional resilience, identifies strengths

RELIEF: Heal limiting beliefs that stem from childhood

PREP TIME: 10 minutes

ACTIVITY TIME: 50 minutes

MATERIALS:
- Journal
- Markers
- Colored Pencils

ACTIVITY HEADNOTE: I first experienced John Bradshaw's Wounded Inner-Child exercise when I participated in Deepak Chopra's and Oprah's Meditation Experience. I found it a powerful way to connect to your inner child. There are many opportunities in my life that I love to connect to my own inner child—roller skating, eating gummy worms, picnics in my backyard, and playing with children. These are definitely pleasant memories of my childhood. However, when we experience traumatic events in our childhood, or if our emotions weren't nurtured, then we can feel disconnected from our inner child. This is an opportunity to connect with your inner child to see if there is a need that can be addressed. Your inner child may have a special message for you. Take some time to find a comfortable seated position.

STEPS:

1. Listen to the guided meditation, or follow the prompt. https://leahguzman.com/resource-guide

2. Here is the prompt: Find yourself a comfortable seated position. Close your eyes, and settle in. Go to the house you grew up in. Look through the window, and find yourself in the house. What do you see? What are you doing? What do you feel is going on with you and your relationships with everyone in that house? What gift did you possess that others overlooked or missed? What burdens did you carry? What brought you hope? What made you sad?

3. Use assorted drawing materials to draw what you saw your inner child doing in the house you grew up in.

4. Answer the questions below.

5. Next, use your non-dominant hand to write a letter from your inner child to yourself now.

QUESTIONS FOR REFLECTION: What does your inner child need? What message does your inner child want you to know? Incorporate this message into your day. What are you not saying that's getting stuck in your throat? What is unprocessed that needs to be articulated? What do you need to say, and to whom?

Manifesting Art Exercises: Throat Chakra

1. DECLARING YOUR TRUTH

BENEFITS: Claims what you want, builds confidence

RELIEF: Changes subconscious beliefs

PREP TIME: 10 minutes

ACTIVITY TIME: 50 minutes

MATERIALS:
Large white paper

- Black paint
- pencil

ACTIVITY HEADNOTE: The importance of declaring your truth of what you want is to match the frequency of your desire. Affirmations can change your subconscious beliefs. When I was starting to exhibit my work online and locally, I had an underlying belief that no one cared about my work. Why was my art important, and why would I do this? This was a lie I was telling myself to stop me from sharing; it was my Ego protecting me so that I would "play small." I created an affirmation that said, "My work is important, powerful, and healing in the world." After seeing this message every day, I was able to change my subconscious belief, and now I truly know my artwork is powerful and important in the world. My art is medicine for my soul and for those who view it. You can create several affirmations. They can relate to finances—"Money flows easily to me"—or your body—"I love my healthy, fit self." I like to keep my affirmations on my phone as daily reminders. That way, I see them daily and accept them as my truth.

STEPS:

- Choose an affirmation that supports your BIG DREAM.
- Use a pencil to sketch out the placement on the paper; do this lightly.
- Then, outline your message with paint.
- Create several affirmations, and hang them around your home.
- When you see the affirmation, say it out loud.
- Here are some examples:
- My great work is financially supported.
- I attract clients who are happy to give me money.
- My artwork is powerful, healing, and important in the world.
- I draw to me divine clients who seek enlightenment through my process. The sharing elevates both of us.
- I know my truth, and I share it.
- My life is guided by divine synchronicity.
- I am guided by my deepest purpose.

NOTE: Be sure your affirmation is in a present-tense form. Also include it as a positive statement. If you wish not to create large-sized paintings of your affirmations, Post-It notes are also an option.

QUESTIONS FOR REFLECTION: How does it feel to speak your desire into the world? Give this time to develop your confidence. The belief of what stopped you took time to develop. Changing your belief will take time, too. I saw shifts happen in my own life within 21 days.

2. TREASURE MAPPING YOUR COURSE

BENEFITS: Increases self-awareness and emotional resilience, identifies strengths

RELIEF: Seeing the big picture to navigate

PREP TIME: 10 minutes

ACTIVITY TIME: 50 minutes

MATERIALS:
- Watercolor paper (or journal)
- Markers
- Pencil
- Assorted paints
- Brushes
- Paint palette
- Water container
- An agenda or planner

ACTIVITY HEADNOTE: The Treasure Map is your game plan. This is an adaptation from Shakti Gawain's book, *Creative Visualization*. To bring your big vision into action, start by creating a visual map. Write out the ideas that you have at the moment to bring your vision to life. I like this exercise because it gives you a visual of the journey. Your map may be of a seascape of islands or a landscape. Choose one area of your life, a specific desire that would have the most ripple effect in your life. It may include a few big projects that are related to the big vision. This is an opportunity to see how your projects and ideas can start to be broken down into smaller steps.

STEPS:

1. Identify three projects/visions that you would like to see happen in the next three months or year.

2. Use symbols to represent the project. Create a "key" to identify the symbols for the project or vision. Place in the corner of the page.

3. Next, draw out the projects as if you were creating a treasure map.

4. Brainstorm all the details that it would need to make it come to life.

5. Break down the steps, and add them to the map.

6. Color or paint the treasure map, so you can see the course.

7. Put the tasks into your journal.

NOTE: Give yourself time to complete your project. You can start on it one day and come back to it another day. When I did this for myself, I didn't include my monthly membership Creative Soul Society group, which I nurture daily. When I gave myself a day to come back to review I and realized I hadn't put it on my list. It made me realize my S.O.S.—"Shiny Object Syndrome"—my habit of thinking that the next new object (or project) is more exciting, rather than focusing and tending to what I have established. I love how my map showed me this and where I needed to focus my attention.

QUESTIONS FOR REFLECTION: Creating a fun visual of your journey helps you see that there may be obstacles along the way. You can draw them in as they show up. Instead of quitting or becoming frustrated and disappointed, think of other ways to figure out the course. What are the steps you need to take to move forward with each project? Write out actionable steps in your agenda that will allow you to start moving forward with your desire.

3. SPARK THE CONVERSATION

BENEFITS: Increases self-awareness and emotional resilience, identifies strengths

RELIEF: Changes subconscious beliefs that hold you back from manifesting

PREP TIME: 10 minutes

ACTIVITY TIME: 50 minutes

MATERIALS:
- Journal
- Pen

ACTIVITY HEADNOTE: You may have a limiting belief about yourself that is not true. It is common to have a limiting belief such as, "I am not good enough," "I might fail," or "I don't feel supported." Our beliefs shape our feelings and actions. Research on shame suggests that one negative comment, such as "You are stupid" will take fourteen positive statements to negate the belief. Your words to yourself have so much power.

What we tell ourselves is what will appear in our lives. Let's program our brain to work for us—not against us. I'm going to list some examples below that are powerful affirmations and invocations for creating change. These should be repeated so that your unconscious mind will accept them as your truth. Conversation *catalyzes*! What is the new story you want to tell yourself and others?

STEPS:

1. Choose statements that resonate with you and support you. These statements are letting The Universe know you are ready to receive. You can choose several.

2. Write your story in your journal. Expand your vision by writing in detail about what you want. Think of everything being reciprocal. If you are attracting clients, think of how excited you are to serve them. Then write their experience of how happy they are to receive your support.

3. Create an image by drawing out what you write as inspiration.

4. Now take this a step further, and share this vision with a friend.

5. Have them expand on your dream.

NOTE: You can even practice this technique when you meet someone new. Let them know who you are as your ideal self. For example, "I'm an international best-selling author supporting millions of creatives to live their dreams."

QUESTIONS FOR REFLECTION: How did it feel to share your vision with someone? How did it feel to have your vision expanded? Did the person you shared your dream with give you suggestions or feedback? Be open to receiving feedback, because it can help chart your course. Who do you need to co-create with to make this happen? Focus on one, and start the steps. You can make a list of contacts to call, schedule an appointment, take the initiative of connecting, and speak about your vision to others.

Chapter 4

HEART CHAKRA

Focus: Giving and Receiving Love

The heart Chakra is located in your chest. In Sanskrit, it is known as *anahata*. The heart is a very intelligent organ, the first to develop in your body. The intention of this Chakra is to overcome separation and division. Our innermost desire is to feel love and connection. Love is the most powerful energy in The Universe. To align with The Universe and co-create, we must love ourselves first. Everything in life is a relationship. We must also take care of all our relationships related to time, money, friends, family, and our own energy. If you can add love to every interaction that you do, it will multiply your manifestation process.

The heart Chakra is located in the exact center of the seven Chakras, with three below and three above. It balances the energy that goes up and the energy that goes down. In order to love, there has to be a letting go of the ego—that will allow greater unity. The balance is still being rooted in order to nourish and provide roots. You need to have an open heart to co-create your desires with others. We will be exploring different relationships that support you in manifesting your desire. We will also explore where your heart needs to be healed in order for it to open up to new experiences and connected to all beings in your life.

FUNCTION: Relates to love, and the inner state is compassion. Chief operating property is equilibrium, finding balance, giving and receiving, finding the flow. It is the sacred marriage of masculine and feminine energy. The heart is the center for peace.

Opening the heart Chakra requires a combination of technique and understanding. We need to look at personal relationships and others around us. The heart requires an understanding and practice of balance—between body and mind, inner and outer realms, self and other, giving and receiving. Opening the heart requires transcendence of the ego, allowing us to surrender to forces larger than the self.

BALANCE: Practice living as if life is *your masterpiece*. Infuse love into everything that you do. Love the way you cook your dinner, the way you decorate your space, fold the clothes, nurture your relationships, smile at the person passing by. Surrender, and let things happen—let things be the way they are. Love is not a matter of getting connected to someone. Love is a matter of seeing that we already are connected within an intricate web of relationships and spiritual connections.

On the other hand, the heart can be blocked by holding grudges, resentment, and grief. We will be exploring several ways to heal the heart. You can lose your alignment if your heart is *too* open. If you give too much and do not replenish your cup with self-care, it will lead to resentments. This would indicate that your Chakra is spinning too fast. You can lose your ground if you give when your energy is depleted. Constant overdrawing of the soil depletes the resources, until we can't give at all. Then we have a backlash. Tending to your heart is about balancing the giving and receiving. Holding resentment stops the flow of energy. The heart can be imbalanced if we live in grievances. Someone may have hurt you, and you are holding on to the pain. You can choose what you want to do with the pain. Some people may choose to hurt the person back. This is not living from the heart. When you encounter hurt feelings from the past or present, choose to feel it fully, and let them go. Letting go is making a choice, and it makes it easier to move on.

The heart Chakra can be blocked by grief. If you have lost loved ones and are carrying the pain in your heart, try the *Healing the Heart* exercise below.

The heart is an intelligent organ. It's the first to develop in the womb, and it's a great communicator. The heart Chakra is the midway point between the lower and upper Chakras. It's incredibly important to listen to your heart and build your life around what you love. When you open your heart, you are connecting to The Universe.

I really love this Chakra. Let's open our heart. Are you continuing with a daily gratitude practice? You can post what you love and are grateful for in the group. By doing this, you are raising your vibration and opening up your relationship with The Universe. Also, say "I love" a lot. This will raise your vibration.

> *"The heart is the originator; your mind is the assistant."*
> ~Sonia Choquette

Imagine that life is like a lightbulb. It's a lot easier to take the cord and plug it into the right socket. But how many times do we insist on trying to plug it into the wrong socket? *I'll try this body, this person, this career.* Not getting very much juice from that, either.

There is one little tiny socket into which we can plug the cord. It's the only one that fits, and it's the only socket wired to bring you the flowing and living waters of grace. That socket dwells in your heart, the very core of your being. How many times each day do we check to see that the cord is still plugged in? How many times do we remember to ask ourselves: Is my commitment to love, or is my commitment to fear?

It's not about the end result. It's about plugging into love and letting love propel it to where it wants to go.

> *"Only from the heart can you touch the sky."*
> ~Rumi

LOCATION: In the heart; its element is air, and its name is *Anahata*.

ELEMENT: Air

INTENTION: The purpose is to find balance in giving and receiving equally.

PHYSICAL ASPECT: Glands: Thymus, other body parts: lungs, heart, pericardium, arms, hands

IMBALANCE: asthma, high blood pressure, heart disease, lung disease

Judgment, jealousy, undue attachment to one person, withholding love, fear of not being accepted can lower the energy of the heart.

SYMBOLS: 12-petal lotus, swords, Venus, copper, touch, antelope, birds, dove, and heart. The element is air—it gives birds the freedom to fly, expansive, spirited. Air implies spaciousness, which is achieved through letting go.

COLOR FREQUENCY: pink and green

AFFIRMATIONS:

I am worthy of Love
I let go of grievances
I let go of resentments
I am opening myself to Love again
I forgive
I live in grace
I live in peace
I am Love

Interview with Flora Bowley

Flora Bowley (pronounced *bowl*-lee) is an artist, author, and gentle guide whose soulful approach to the creative process has touched thousands of lives.

Blending more than twenty years of professional painting experience with her background as a yoga instructor, healer, and lifelong truth seeker, Flora's intimate in-person workshops and popular online courses have empowered a global network of brave painters, while creating a new holistic movement in the intuitive art world.

More recently, Flora's creative passions have led her to explore the vast ways in which the principles of creativity can serve as fuel for a more alive and awakened way of living in the world—no paintbrushes required.

www.florabowley.com

LEAH: Flora, the biggest impression you have on me is your heart-centered practice and building your global community. You've also experienced grief and included it in your art practice. This work is about experiencing all of these emotions and embracing them.

I would love to discuss your learning lessons, challenges, insight, and wisdom along your artistic journey.

LEAH: Can you please start us off at the beginning of your artistic journey, as an artist and entrepreneur?

FLORA: I loved making art as a kid, and, thankfully, my family encouraged it. I was also that kid trying to sell weird clay pots or seaweed jewelry to the neighbors because I thought being able to make money from what I loved to do was fun. That said, I never had any big blocks around the commercial piece of being an artist. That said, I also didn't grow up thinking I could be a professional, working artist. I didn't have any role models who were doing that, so I went to college thinking I would study interior or graphic design.

However, that all changed pretty quickly after my first painting class. I was hooked. I couldn't get enough of the medium, and eventually, I started hanging my work in places like hair salons and coffee shops. After a few dedicated years of painting, I started showing my work in galleries. I also became a yoga instructor and massage therapist to support my art dreams.

When I eventually did start squeaking by as a full-time painter (what I thought was my dream job), I realized I was actually quite lonely painting away in my studio all day. I craved community, but I wasn't sure what that meant or what that would look like. After a year of soul searching, a friend of mine suggested I start teaching painting. Quickly after that seed was planted, I was invited to teach at an art retreat, and, within hours of sharing my process, I realized *this* was actually my dream job. I loved witnessing other people wake up to their creativity. That was more than a decade ago, and I've been doing it ever since.

I've learned so much by sharing my intuitive painting process with others, but perhaps the most potent takeaway is how the creative process can support a more alive and awake way of living. This is what my latest book, *The Art of Aliveness*, is all about.

LEAH: For manifesting, what relationships and connections did you make that helped shape you as an entrepreneur? Any special connections or experiences that helped you bring your vision into reality?

FLORA: Squam Art Workshops was the first place I ever shared my painting process, and that experience really connected me to so many wonderful people and opportunities. An author scout actually attended my workshop, so that led to writing my first book, *Brave Intuitive Painting*, in the year following my first class. I believe when we're doing what we're supposed to be doing and coming from a place of service, opportunities tend to present themselves, which has definitely been true for me.

I also *love* people and have a very collaborative spirit, which definitely helps!

LEAH: What obstacles and challenges did you experience?

FLORA: My life has been very blessed in many ways, but I've also made a lot of choices that have gotten me where I am now. For example, I lived very simply for a long time—squatting illegally in art studios or living with big groups of people to make ends meet as an artist. I put my art first, which, for me, meant *not* doing a lot of things society expects, like having children, getting married, or working a "regular" job. I love my life, but there have certainly been sacrifices along the way.

Losing my mom to cancer six years ago was also an incredibly difficult and impactful experience for me—one that has informed everything about my life since.

LEAH: How did art help you heal during this challenging time?

FLORA: Painting has proven to be one of the most potent ways to process grief. It allows me to move what is stirring inside and actually get it out of my body and onto the canvas. I also do a lot of dancing while I paint, so it becomes a really cathartic somatic experience. Sometimes I start paintings by writing letters to my mom—big, loopy letters on the canvas which eventually become buried in the layers of paint. Angel forms often show up, which also makes me feel connected to my mom.

I believe one of the greatest gifts of the creative process is that it gives us a way to move things *through*.

LEAH: Can you tell us more about your principles of creativity and how they fuel you and your community for a more alive, awakened life (even without paintbrushes)?

FLORA: Yes! It's an exciting leap for me to explore the principles of creativity and how they apply to living without painting being at the forefront of the experience. My new book, *The Art of Aliveness,* is all about how our lives can become our greatest works of art and how creativity can support this.

One of the foundational pieces in my approach to painting is that I don't have a plan going in. Instead of trying to execute an idea from my head, I just begin by adding marks and moving colors across the canvas. Painting in this way becomes a "presence practice," because it requires moment-to-moment honesty and re-evaluation as things come and go. It's a juicy metaphor for living, because, while plans can be helpful, we never really know what the future holds, and creativity teaches us to be open to change and ready to pivot at any moment. The more we do this on the canvas, the stronger those muscles become in life.

I also talk a lot about "Working with what's working." This guiding principle is quite contrary to a typical art-school critique, where you're encouraged to look for what's *not* working. I've learned over the years that most people are naturally oriented to look for what's *not* working, both in life and in painting, so I try to change this lens. By focusing on one thing that might be "working," whether it's a mark or color, or one area of a painting (or of your life), the path forward comes into focus much more easily. When you look only for what's *not* working, it's easy to just feel stuck.

Another chapter in my book is called, "Contrast is Crucial." In art-making processes, contrast brings vitality and spark to a piece of art by creating push and pull. On the other hand, if you stay in what I call "midtown," everything feels similar, and you lose the pop. Again, this is the same in life. When we fall too deeply into habitual patterns, we move away from our aliveness, but when we actively choose to create contrast by mixing things up and staying open to new experiences and possibilities, we ultimately feel more alive.

LEAH: Do you have any words of wisdom to give the artists who are starting their journey and wanting to come out to share their gifts with the world?

FLORA: The world is changing so quickly, and I really believe we need all the artists and healers to step into their gifts. It can be easy to think what you have to offer is not worthy or important, but I disagree. Start by making time each day to get quiet and get acquainted with your intuitive voice. I believe that voice is your soul whispering (or sometimes yelling) instructions for how to move forward. Trust those voices, and keep noticing what makes you feel the most alive. Like Howard Thurman said, "Don't ask yourself what the world needs. Ask yourself what makes you come alive, and go do that, because what the world needs is people who have come alive."

Your gifts are worthy and needed.

Personal Story

I love how Flora encourages us to stay alive by trusting our intuition, following our heart and sharing our gifts with the world. Even if you can't see the whole path, trust the process. The Universe is guiding you in the right direction.

In one of my group sessions in the Creative Soul Society, we focused on the heart Chakra and created the Heart Strings, with the intention of *Who do we need to bring into our lives to work on our desires?* As you create the art, you may get ideas. It's important to listen to your intuition. One of my visions is to see art therapy in schools across America giving the students an outlet to express themselves through art in a safe space. For one of my strings, I wrote to the First Lady, Dr. Jill Biden. I felt I needed to reach a heartfelt person who would have connections to make this happen. That night I wrote a letter to Dr. Biden in my journal. A month later, I created my vision board, keeping in mind my big vision. I didn't find an image of Dr. Biden, but I did find one of Michelle Obama. A few weeks passed, and I kept thinking how I would connect with these powerful, smart, inspiring women to let them know of my mission. I was scrolling through my news feed, and Barack Obama and Michelle Obama's home showed up. It was a beautiful tour, and the editor of the article included their address! I couldn't believe it! The Universe kept giving me clues. I knew my art was giving me the message with the image. Now I knew I had to send Michelle Obama my *Essential Art Therapy Exercises* book, letting her know of my vision. The part that is important here is, even though I followed the signs, I let go of the outcome. I didn't expect a response. Who knew if she would really ever receive my letter and book? The important part about this story is that I've surrendered my vision to The Universe. I was just given the signs, and I followed them. I let The Universe take care of the details. It showed that I'm connected, and I trust the clues came to me for a reason. Since I put my intention out into the world I've had opportunities to present to school districts about the mental health benefits of art therapy in schools.

Meditation: Heart Chakra Meditation Link:

https://leahguzman.com/resource-guide

- Close your eyes.
- Breathe in through your nose and out through your mouth.
- Focus your attention on your heart center.
- Place your hands on your heart.
- Breathe into your heart.
- Feel and see a beautiful white light.
- Spread the white light, glowing, shimmering around your body.
- This is the light of love; love is your essence.
- Let this love radiate to fill the room you are in; let it fill the space.
- Radiate the love to all your friends and family.
- You are a generator of love.
- They feel your love.
- They are generators of love.
- The love is a circuit board, and all the hearts are connected, radiating love.
- We are lighting up, radiating light.
- The love is reaching all the continents; it encompasses the Earth.
- Your love is expansive, connecting throughout The Universe.
- The message of your heart is: *You are brilliant, you are loved, you are complete.*
- Breathe in deeply; open your eyes.

"Love is a currency; whatever you give will come back to you."
~Leah Guzman

Strengthening tools for the Heart Chakra:

1. Wear the color green. Green brings the color of harmony, reliability, and balance. It's associated with the heart Chakra. When the Chakra is balanced, it brings feelings of love, compassion, healing, and connection. The Chakra can become imbalanced by grief. Wear the color green; carry jade and green stones to help balance this Chakra.

2. Carry the stones: green tourmaline, emerald, malachite, jade, rose quartz, or kunzite

3. Smile at everyone you see daily. Even if you don't like smiling, it's contagious.

4. Give family and friends positive compliments and feedback.

5. Give silent blessings.

6. Give a gift.

7. Forgive and move on.

8. Essential Oils: Rose and Pine.

9. Try to go for one day without criticizing or complaining about anyone or anything.

AFFIRMATIONS:

I am loving and lovable.
I am a source of healing in the world.
I am deeply compassionate.

Healing Art Exercises: Heart Chakra

1. HEALING HEART MANDALA

BENEFITS: Increases self-awareness and emotional resilience

RELIEF: Heals resentments, grief, and disconnection

PREP TIME: 10 minutes

ACTIVITY TIME: 50 minutes

MATERIALS:
- Journal
- Pen or pencil
- Colored pencils—green and pink

ACTIVITY HEADNOTE: Opening your heart takes time, especially if you are experiencing grief or resentment. Listening to your heart can bring in so much healing. Self-compassion is one of our biggest tools for bringing in love. We are here to love, it's the strongest frequency in The Universe. This exercise will help you heal your heart. It will also give you the strength to open up your heart to allow new relationships to form in manifesting what you desire.

STEPS:

1. Start with the heart-centered meditation. https://leahguzman.com/resource-guide
2. Draw a circle with a pencil.
3. Draw another circle around the first circle.
4. Write things you love in between the two circles.
5. Add the 12-petal lotus to your design.
6. Continue to add details.
7. Add the Chakra healing colors green and pink.
8. Use the black-ink pen to outline.
9. Add the affirmations that resonate with you: *I am worthy of Love, I let go of grievances, I let go of resentments, I am opening myself to Love again, I forgive, I live in grace, I live in peace, I am Love.*

NOTE: You can do this as a group of people who have all lost a loved one. Healing heart mandala can be done with everyone working together on one large canvas.

QUESTIONS FOR REFLECTION: If it is difficult to write, "I forgive" or even "I love," then honor where you're at right now. You can write instead, "I'm learning to love myself."

"I'm moving toward forgiving to heal myself"—not for what the other person did that was wrong, but to heal yourself from the pain. Are there any other resentments about which you feel you need to clear the air in your life?

"In the garden of life, friends are the flowers."
~Leah Guzman

2. HEART PAINTING WITH SYMBOLS

BENEFITS: Increases self-awareness and emotional resilience, identifies strengths

RELIEF: Grief, resentments

PREP TIME: 10 minutes

ACTIVITY TIME: 50 minutes

MATERIALS:
- Small canvas (4" x 4" or 6" x 6")
- Pencil
- Acrylic paint (white, green, pink)
- Brushes
- Paint palette
- Water container
- Paper towel
- Black pen (fine-point marker)

ACTIVITY HEADNOTE: I've been offering heart-painting workshops for years. I find it interesting to see how the heart is expressed visually. I've seen broken, winged, caged, anchored, and bleeding hearts, to name a few. This is an opportunity to check in with your heart to see what is resonating with it. Universal symbol of the heart means that most cultures agree that the heart is the symbol for love. There is not a specific date when the heart was first used to signify "love," but it has been used for centuries.

THE ART OF HEALING AND MANIFESTING

STEPS:

1. Draw a large circle on the canvas. Or you can use the whole canvas for your image.

2. Look up an image of a heart online (use Universal or anatomical image).

3. Looking at the image, draw your own version on the canvas inside the circle with pencil.

4. Add paint to fill in space.

5. Next, once the paint is dry. use the black-ink pen to fill in the heart.

6. Add your heart affirmation: *I am loving and lovable. I am a source of healing in the world. I am deeply compassionate.*

7. Place your canvas on the wall to view daily.

NOTE: If you are holding resentment toward a person, forgive them. Forgiving them does not excuse their wrong actions—it allows your self to heal.

QUESTIONS FOR REFLECTION: Where in your life can you open your heart a little more?

3. OPENING THE HEART WITH SERVICE

BENEFITS: Increases empathy and emotional resilience

RELIEF: Opens the heart, processes grief and resentment

PREP TIME: 10 minutes

ACTIVITY TIME: 50 minutes

MATERIALS:
- Small canvas (4" x 4" or 6" x 6")
- Pencil
- Acrylic paint (white, indigo blue, silver, or gold)
- Brushes
- Paint palette
- Water container
- Paper towel
- Black pen (fine-point marker)

ACTIVITY HEADNOTE: Have you heard of the concept "give what you want to receive?" If you want love, give love. If you want money, give money. If you want praise, give praise. For healing the heart, it's important to move the energy. Being of service is an excellent way to heal yourself and help others. The healing of the heart is about giving and receiving equally. An imbalanced Chakra would show up when you are being stingy with giving—or the opposite, over-giving. Over-giving leads to resentment. This is about finding the balance to create flow in your life. The heart Chakra is about what you can give. As part of my business, I give monthly to a charity. It feels really good to give back.

STEPS:

1. Choose one way to be of service to someone; act selflessly (this can be in the form of a gift, silent blessing, a phone call to see how someone is doing, donating to charity, etc.).

2. Choose one way you can ask for help in your manifestation process.

3. Draw out ways you can give and receive to keep your heart Chakra open.

QUESTIONS FOR REFLECTION: How did it feel to give without expectation? Unconditional love is a beautiful lesson to learn in life. In what areas are you loving unconditionally (for example, a pet or family member)?

Manifesting Art Exercises: Heart Chakra

1. HEART CONNECTIONS

BENEFITS: Increases self-awareness and emotional resilience, identifies strengths

RELIEF: Anxiety, Depression, PTSD

PREP TIME: 10 minutes

ACTIVITY TIME: 50 minutes

MATERIALS:
- Printed heart (anatomical or draw your own)
- Journal
- Assorted drawing and painting media

ACTIVITY HEADNOTE: **Heart connection exercise** is an opportunity to dream big and call in the connections you need to manifest your dream. Go ahead and stretch yourself. Even if you don't know how it's going to work out, make the plan anyway. For example, I wanted to remodel my house—actually add an extension for my dream studio. I actually called in a contractor to give me some estimates. Next, I learned that I needed to call in an architect to design it. Let your art speak to you and guide you. Even if you don't feel that you're ready yet, take the first baby step.

STEPS:

1. Print image of heart.

2. Identify all the relationships and people you will need to bring into your life to make your desire happen.

3. Who do you need to connect with to manifest your desire?

4. Make connecting strings radiating out of the heart; each string represents a person.

NOTE: If you have doubts or resistance to calling in people before you're ready, ask The Universe to support you. The people you need might already be in your orbit.

QUESTIONS FOR REFLECTION: How does it feel to be expansive? Schedule the time to make the connection with the people you are calling in to support you.

2. DREAM TEAM

BENEFITS: Increases self-awareness

RELIEF: Support for making your vision a reality

PREP TIME: 10 minutes

ACTIVITY TIME: 50 minutes

MATERIALS:
- Journal
- Assorted drawing materials

ACTIVITY HEADNOTE: As you gain awareness of who you need to call in to make the connections, start creating your Dream Team. This idea has been adapted from the *Creating on Purpose* book. If you have kids at home and need support with housecleaning or a sitter, think about who could be available for you. If you need someone to brainstorm your marketing or help you post, call in an assistant. I have called in many people to help support me on my journey. One in particular is my accountability partner, whom I meet with weekly to review the steps I have been taking toward my desire. You don't have to meet your person in person. It can be done through video chat or on the phone. When you meet with your partner, keep it very clear and related to what you want to manifest. What I've learned from having an accountability partner for more than five years is that I must follow through with what I say I'm going to do. When I first started out, I would think I needed to complete a task to make sure I had followed through for our meeting. Even if I didn't follow through, it was a sign that that may not be the direction I needed to go in or that I had an underlying limiting belief to explore. The practice of meeting an accountability partner builds confidence to trusting yourself and following through with what you say.

STEPS:

1. Make a list of all the places in your life in which you need support.

2. Identify what person would be able to help you (examples include financial planner, housekeeper, assistant, accountability partner, babysitter, web designer).

3. Draw out a circle.

4. Create lines on your diagram with your list of support areas.

5. Ask The Universe for support.

6. Take a step today to ask for help from a friend, or research online.

NOTE: Your friends are excellent resources for finding referrals. I've found assistance in Facebook groups just by asking for help.

QUESTIONS FOR REFLECTION: How does it feel to be supported? This is an opportunity to write what it feels like to have all the support you need to make your desire come to life, whether it's running a business, putting together an art show, or managing your home life.

3. AMPLIFY MANIFESTING WITH BEAUTY

BENEFITS: Increases self-awareness and emotional resilience, identifies strengths

RELIEF: Relieves stress by focusing on the things that light you up.

PREP TIME: 10 minutes

ACTIVITY TIME: 50 minutes

MATERIALS:
- Journal
- Assorted Drawing Materials

ACTIVITY HEADNOTE: What in your life is beautiful? It may be watching the sunset, how've you decorated your space, or looking at a child's face. What do you love specifically about the dream you are manifesting? Is it the idea of freedom? Is it being in creative flow? Is it helping others? Is it your client's face when they experience transformation or have your art in their home? This exercise is about raising your vibration.

When you are in the space of gratitude, beauty, and love, you are in direct connection with Source energy.

STEPS:

1. Choose something of beauty in your life today that you would like to honor.

2. Notice the beauty around you in nature, in the food you eat, in how you dress.

3. Create an image of beauty in your journal.

4. Use assorted art media.

QUESTIONS FOR REFLECTION: How can you create beauty in your living space? How about in the way you dress? What areas of your life hold beauty right now? What in your life right now is working well?

Chapter 5

SOLAR PLEXUS CHAKRA

Focus: Building Willpower and Purpose

*T*he intention of the solar plexus Chakra is to attain personal power. We want to use power to enhance, empower, and strengthen our lives. We want to tap into power with purpose. In Sanskrit, it is known as *manipura* or "lustrous gem." The third Chakra is related to willpower, assertiveness, inner state of laughter, joy, and anger. It is located around the navel in the area of the solar plexus and up to the breastbone. One of the symbols is fire. Fire is radiant and also brings transformation. Think about a forest being burned, in order to clear the ground to create better-quality soil and allow new growth to emerge. This Chakra controls metabolism and digestion. Again, this is about processing and moving the energy—just like the function of your stomach. Most clients I have worked with need healing in this Chakra for transformation and alignment to occur. Do you feel worthy of your desires? This is about building your self-esteem, creating boundaries, learning how to say "No" to things that don't light you up, and believing in yourself. We need to listen to our gut feelings.

BALANCED: When your solar Chakra is balanced, you will feel light, energetic, and powerful, and you will have vitality.

We have to put in energy to get back energy; you have created everything in your life at this moment. We have to keep in touch with what is best for us. Let's ask ourselves, "What is my service to the world, and how can I best offer this to the world?"

As you step into sharing your amazing creative gifts with others, you will undoubtedly stumble, fall down, and learn how to get right back up. This is resilience. Through our mess-ups, we can get clear about what we really want. See it as a stepping stone—it's a part of the journey. You have to lose more to win more. Confidence is learning to trust yourself. This Chakra is about building your self-confidence and boundaries, and learning to say "No" to things that don't align with your big dream.

IMBALANCED: ulcers, diabetes, hypoglycemia, digestive disorders, metabolism, physically tight, hard stomachs, large potbellies, or sunken diaphragm. Large bellies may indicate an excessive need to be in power, to dominate and control or simply an egotistical need to take up space. A weak, sunken Chakra indicates fear of taking power, a withdrawal into the self, or a fear of standing out.

When your solar plexus is imbalanced, you may feel anger and a lack of willpower or self-control. If the Chakra is spinning too fast, the person may be overbearing, domineering, and controlling. If the Chakra is spinning too slow, then they may lack confidence or self-worth and have feelings of shame.

Anger and resentment can block this Chakra. You may need to clear this Chakra by drawing out your anger (anger monster) to set it free. When you learn to let go of resentment and forgive, things in your life that no longer serve you will naturally fade away.

The theme of this Chakra is "Moving to the *True You*." This is where we let go of limiting beliefs, take aligned action, and focus on what we really want to manifest in order to make our desires come into reality. The solar plexus is radiant, just like you. We want to identify our strengths, turn on our superpowers, and stand tall!

Okay, so what are the steps? In every decision that you make, you will need to check in with yourself to see if it aligns with your purpose (desires). Does the decision feed your soul, or does it deplete you? Listen to your body. Is it physically leaning into taking that new course, following that new path? It may seem scary to follow our dreams, yet it's good to feel uncomfortable and do it *anyway*.

When we start taking the steps toward our true self, our authentic self, we will start shining bright like a lustrous gem.

PHYSICAL ASPECT: Body parts: digestive system, muscles

COLOR FREQUENCY: Yellow

ELEMENT: Fire

SYMBOLS: Ram, fire, ten-petal lotus, yellow color, energy (combustion), sun, Mars, or butterfly.

AFFIRMATIONS:

I love and accept myself.
I am strong and courageous.
I am authentic.
I am free to choose any situation.
I feel my own power.
I choose healthy relationships.
I am worthy of love, kindness, and respect.

Personal Story:

Here's a situation that showed up for me. I had a co-worker who was constantly triggering me. The trigger was that they continued to piss me off, challenged my knowledge, and tried to control me and tell me what to do. This definitely brought feelings of anger and resentment. Around this same time, I chose that I would no longer be a people pleaser. I stood my ground and said "No" to requests that did not resonate with me. Most people want to blame the other person for causing a negative reaction within them. I admit that I did this. The truth is that the person who is behaving this way needs a lot of healing themselves. But before we place all the blame on the other person, let's look at ourselves first. We need to question why this person is triggering us. What is happening that makes me feel threatened and angry? Anger is one of the signs of the solar-plexus Chakra needing balancing. It's a sign to strengthen your own self-confidence and heal the inner anger, in order to change the relationship with this person. It's also triggering the Ego to want to be "right." It's a true power struggle for control. I could physically feel the energy in my stomach. I felt nauseous around the person.

I had to first acknowledge that this was happening. My first response was to make art about it. What did this energy look like for me? It was daggers to my solar plexus.

Another thought was *I need to get a new job (just to avoid this person)*. Yet, running from the situation rarely fixes the problem. More than likely, when you find the new job, the situation will occur again. That's how The Universe works. If you haven't learned a particular lesson, it will give you another opportunity to experience it. I had to do the work of healing myself by identifying my own Ego wounds, building my self-confidence, and then energetically sending love to this person who despised me.

I used several techniques to protect my energy. When I was near the person, I would not face them directly, shielding my solar plexus. I imagined a white light around me for protection, and I carried a citrine crystal. Using a variety of tools for healing is beneficial. One of the most powerful ones for me—one I could physically feel a difference from—was practicing a cord-cutting meditation. The process is a guided meditation of visually cutting cords that were energetically harming me. Everyone we meet has a thin energy cord connecting us. Some cords can get tangled. You can visualize cutting any cords that are not serving you. As you do this, you can send the person love. Thank the person for showing you that you also needed healing. Forgive them for causing you pain (you can practice my cord-cutting meditation if you need support). Once I was able to heal the resistance within myself, the person no longer showed up in my life. The Universe magically changed their schedule, so I wouldn't have to see them ever again. Hallelujah! I was incredibly grateful I had done the work, and it magically released the person from my world.

However, within the next year, I met a very similar person with the same personality. I knew this was a test. Being in the room with this person did not trigger me. I knew right away that I would not respond the same way as before. I chose to respond with love and non-reaction. When I was able to not use my Ego to respond to this challenging personality and responded instead with love and acceptance, I was free from the controlling behavior. I could see the lesson I needed to learn, and I learned it! I was actually thrilled that I no longer was triggered and thanked The Universe for giving me this lesson. I share this story with you because, when we experience resistance, it's a blessing in disguise. Lean into it. Dive deeper to discover what needs to be healed within you. Each of the Chakras we review have an imbalance if you are experiencing the uncomfortable feelings associated with that particular Chakra. Then, do the work to heal yourself.

If we do not acknowledge our feelings of resistance, they can manifest into physical symptoms in the body, actually causing pain. This is why it's important to process our emotions. We are now going to explore the Chakras on a deeper level to see the overlapping of emotions, resistance, and how it relates to our body and lives. As you go through this book and feel resistance or pain in your body, take it as a sign, and acknowledge it. There is a gift in its message. Here is a way to address it: "I see/feel you. I acknowledge you. I love you. I listen to you. What message do you have for me? Thank you." Try to see how it works for you.

Interview with Ekaterina Popova:

Ekaterina Popova is an artist who believes that our entire life is a canvas and that we have the power to create anything we desire. Her mission is to empower artists and give them the tools to take responsibility for their own career and find validation and success from within.

Ekaterina spent the past decade growing her painting practice and focusing on depicting the interior in a series of lush and colorful paintings. These works helped her explore and heal her relationship with the idea of "home," which carries a wide array of emotions for humans, especially immigrants. The works have been recognized, exhibited, and published internationally.

Kat is the Founder of *Create! Magazine*, Create! Podcast, and the Art Queens. She also released a book called *Smartist Guide* for artists.

www.ekaterinapopova.com

LEAH: How did you step into your power as an artist?

EKATERINA: When I was younger, when I would think about a stereotypical boss or CEO, I would think of a ruthless, controlling, or maybe even harsh persona. Of course, this was based on the way bosses are portrayed in the media and my own limited experience. Yet, that was never me, which is why I have never considered a leadership position for myself. I have been an introvert and empath my entire life. As a kid, I was painfully shy and a people pleaser. I definitely had a lot of mindset work and healing to do to overcome my past and enable me to get to where I am today.

I still feel I have miles to go, but I have been able to achieve so much, despite past conditioning. To step into my authentic power, I had to listen to the inner whispers. These are gentle nudges that call us to share our story, start a new project we may not feel qualified for, or step into a leadership role.

After working with my coach, Michele Gomez, I learned to look at the best version of myself and ask, "Who do you want to be? What does your work look like? What does your career look like? What does success look like for you? How can you move a tiny inch or centimeter closer to this?"

Stepping into our power also means knowing we're worthy of our desires. What often stops us is self-doubt, self-sabotage, negative, fearful thoughts, discounting our desires, and not taking action due to these fears and blocks. We often stop ourselves before we give something a try, because we think, *Oh, it's not practical. Oh, it's too much. I'm not skilled. I don't know how to do that.* The magical part of stepping into our power is imagining the person you want to be and taking steps to get there.

LEAH: How have you used your art to help you heal?

EKATERINA: My childhood had some turbulent moments. Growing up in post-Soviet Russia with a single mom and later moving to the U.S., I had to find something to keep me grounded. Art created a safe place for me and allowed me to process my experiences. When I was younger, I didn't think I would use my art to talk about safety and belonging. I didn't know why I was painting. I was naturally creating and following the next obvious step. I was making my own space and repainting the story of my childhood, where I didn't feel safe. I didn't have my own room, and I hadn't felt at home for the longest time. Then moving to another country added a whole other layer. Looking back, I can see how healing this was, yet, when I was starting out, I had no idea what I was doing.

LEAH: What was the biggest shift for you?

EKATERINA: The shift came from a place of deep disappointment and self-sabotage. I was sick of my patterns that kept me insecure, broke, and small. I no longer was able to tolerate the person in the mirror. I slowly started showing up daily on social media. I put my art and offers out there for sale. I didn't care if I looked silly or like an amateur. I didn't care if I annoyed people. Finally, I made a decision to show up for myself. It got more accessible and easier as I met amazing, like-minded people who responded to my art and message on a deep level.

LEAH: How did you go from random day jobs to living your dream?

EKATERINA: I kept trying to find a day job that I could tolerate, but I kept felt so wrong about any job I took. One day, I decided to figure out how to become my own boss.

My biggest tip for that is to listen to yourself and your intuition. Everything you do reflects who you are, not just your craft, your business, or your work, but *you* as a person, as a being. So, what I did was to tell myself, "Okay, this is my last three months working here. I'm going to be the best freaking call-center worker!"

I channeled my energy into believing it. Then, on my breaks, I would work on my business. It kept me busy, and it gave me deep gratification knowing that I was supporting my co-workers. In terms of taking the risk and learning when to fly on your own, it's great to have savings and familiar systems for your mental sanity, so that you know you can generate the revenue when you need it.

I learned that, no matter how prepared we are, things will still happen that are out of our control. If you feel called to be your own boss, you will have to take a leap of faith figure it out at some point. There is always a way. I like to play "worst-case scenario games," because I know if I go there mentally, I face my fears and make decisions from love. Then I can focus on the best-case scenario.

I was able to build an art career over time that eventually led to a six-figure business that makes me leap out of bed and want to work on every morning. It was my story to be an example of the fact that you can overcome, too.

LEAH: What techniques do you use to step into your most powerful self?

EKATERINA: We have to keep moving and sharing our truth, trusting that what is meant for us will not pass us. So, it's safe to share your voice. It's safe to share parts of your journey that are less perfect or less polished. Instagram is a fantastic place to start. Before I show up, I do a little meditation. I usually pray and ask for God and angels to speak through me. It sounds silly, yet it's an empowering way to channel your gifts. I like writing the captions out with pen and paper and with love and intention before posting on Instagram. It's about becoming the best version of yourself.

I'm a big fan of affirmations. When I walk my dog, I will say the affirmations to myself. Sometimes I say them out loud, and maybe someone walking by will think I'm crazy. I say things like, "I'm a high-level artist. My work is of high service, and I deserve to be paid hundreds of thousands of dollars."

Another way to step into your power is to start saying "Yes" to activities that scare you a little bit. For me, it was public speaking. It was terrifying for me to use my voice when I was a child, so I had to heal that part of me.

Create your own opportunities. This helps you step into the next level. Invite someone you admire on Instagram live, interview them, start your own blog, create an exhibition—anything where you're in charge. Show yourself that you're capable of creating what you desire. It's the most empowering feeling in the world! Then continue challenging yourself by pushing the quality and boldness of your work. For example, I'm stepping into six-foot canvases and taking up space where I didn't feel safe to take up space before.

The biggest question I ask myself every day is, "How do I want to feel when I get up? What kind of work do I want to create? How do I want to be validated right now?" Sometimes we don't have enough sales, or we don't have enough clients, and we need to ask The Universe, "Hey, can you validate me? I want to see that I'm on the right path to do this type of work. Can you show me?" I just said that to myself two weeks ago. I hadn't sold art in a while, and I felt I would love to sell some art. You can write a pretend letter from a dream client: "Thank you so much for changing my life. Thank you for helping me heal. Thank you for the beautiful art you created." The question that keeps coming up is *How much do you want to earn, and where do you want to earn it from?*

In college, I would listen to Nicki Minaj or Drake and get myself hyped up before class so I would be able to channel into my power. It sounds silly, but that really helped me talk through my fears and insecurities. Now I have a playlist for making money, one for speaking with clients, and one for public speaking.

"Your art matters. Art is not a part of life. It is not an addition to life. It is the essence of those pieces of us that make us fulfilled. That give us hope. That give us dreams and provide the world a view very different than what it would have been without us."
~Hasan Davi

Strengthening Tools for the Solar Plexus Chakra

1. Journal exercise: Release all your letdowns and disappointments.

2. Accept and love all aspects of who you are—even your mistakes.

3. Wear the color yellow. Yellow is enthusiasm, opportunity, and positivity. It relates to the Solar Plexus Chakra. When you are balanced, you will feel powerful,

purposeful, and energetic. If you are imbalanced, you will lack energy. You will be controlling, striving for perfection, and blocked by anger. It relates to low self-esteem and low self-confidence.

4. Carry the stones: Amber or Citrine

5. Scents: Eucalyptus, Lemongrass, Lavender, Ylang yang, Myrrh, Black Pepper

6. Affirmations: I can do anything I set my mind to. I have a good sense of humor and laugh often. I am powerful and use power wisely.

Healing Art Exercises: Solar Plexus Chakra

1. SOLAR PLEXUS MANDALA

BENEFITS: Increases self-awareness and emotional resilience, identifies strengths

RELIEF: Rewires your subconscious mind to let go of limiting beliefs

PREP TIME: 10 minutes

ACTIVITY TIME: 50 minutes

MATERIALS:
- Journal
- Pencil
- Assorted drawing media: Colored pencils, gel pens, or markers (various shades of yellow and gold)
- Black-ink pen

ACTIVITY HEADNOTE: Where in your life do you feel you may be giving away your power? Is it at a work meeting where you aren't speaking up? Are you are pricing your work too low and not charging enough? Is it with your time and not creating boundaries? Do you feel like a victim?

As you realize that your superpower is in your creations, let people know how it benefits them. Let them know that you are providing a service that benefits humanity. If you follow through on your words, your self-esteem builds. Follow through on imagining a bigger dream, speaking your desires, connecting with those who support you. It will help you in creating the life that you want. In this mandala, identify if you are "playing small" in some area, whether it's not showing your art, not taking time to create, or not sharing your gifts in some way. Include it in the mandala, and include the affirmations to empower yourself.

STEPS:

1. Start with the solar plexus *True You* meditation: https://leahguzman.com/resource-guide

2. Draw a circle with a pencil.

3. Draw another circle around the first circle.

4. Write areas of your life where you want to stand your power in between the two circles.

5. Add the ten-petal lotus to your design.

6. Continue to add details.

7. Add the Chakra healing colors of yellow.

8. Use the black-ink pen to outline.

9. Add the affirmations that resonate with you: *I can do anything I set my mind to achieve. I have a good sense of humor and laugh often. I am powerful and use power wisely.*

NOTE: Many creatives have a fear of being judged when they show up in their power. Yes, you will be judged. There are always haters out there. Even Mother Teresa had haters, and she was one of the most-selfless persons who ever lived. When you stand in your power, you are no longer looking for approval outside of yourself. As you are following your path, moving in the direction of your soul, you will feel satisfied.

QUESTIONS FOR REFLECTION: How does it feel to stand in your power? Were you scared at first? How can you plan stepping into your power throughout the day? Share your service and art in our Creative Soul Online Retreat Community.

2. SOLAR PLEXUS PAINTING WITH SYMBOLS

BENEFITS: Increases self-awareness and emotional resilience, identifies strengths

RELIEF: Releases anger that can imbalance this chakra

PREP TIME: 10 minutes

ACTIVITY TIME: 50 minutes

MATERIALS:
- Small canvas (4" x 4" or 6" x 6")
- Pencil
- Acrylic paint (include white and a variety of yellows)
- Brushes
- Paint palette
- Water container
- Paper towel
- Black pen (fine-point marker)
- Print one symbol: Ram, fire, ten-petaled lotus, yellow color, energy (combustion), sun, Mars, or butterfly.

ACTIVITY HEADNOTE: In this painting, you are using the symbols of the Chakra to strengthen your willpower. If you are feeling blocked by anger, I would recommend

using the symbol fire to represent the emotion. Fire can also represent a symbol for regrowth. If you are coming into your power and feel that you are transforming, then a butterfly would be more suited for you. The sun represents shining your light. The ram is a totem animal for the solar plexus chakra and is associated with action, determination, and initiative.

STEPS:

1. Choose an image from the Internet for the solar plexus Chakra.

2. Draw a circle to start or use the entire canvas.

3. Sketch out design on canvas (choose a symbol that relates to your healing).

4. Use the color yellow predominantly in the painting for the outside circle (you can add other colors).

5. Block in colors.

6. Once the canvas is dry, add affirmations to painting. *I am strong and courageous. I am authentic. I am free to choose any situation. I feel my own power. I choose healthy relationships.*

7. Hang the painting with the other paintings in your chakra set.

NOTE: There isn't a wrong way to create this painting. Just choose your intention of what the painting will be about and match it with a symbol.

QUESTIONS FOR REFLECTION: Ask yourself: Do you know what your purpose is in this world? How does living on purpose feel like? How does it feel to stand in you power? What characteristics do you need to embody to bring in your powerful self?

3. REFLECTING ON AVATARS

BENEFITS: Increases self-awareness and emotional resilience, identifies strengths

RELIEF: Becoming aware of where you need to focus your attention

PREP TIME: 10 minutes

ACTIVITY TIME: 50 minutes

MATERIALS:

- Your images of the avatars (your ideal self and the block drawing created earlier in the book).

ACTIVITY HEADNOTE: This exercise is about reflecting on the two avatars you created, your Ideal Self and your block. Place them side by side. Which one of the avatars are you going to give attention to? Ask this question as you move throughout your day. Am I making choices that align with what I want to manifest? What do I need to let go of in my life in order to manifest my desire? Do you need to let go of fear, lack of self-confidence, or a story that is no longer serving you? Is it a toxic relationship, a negative thought, or clutter?

STEPS:

1. Place the two avatars next to each other.

2. Identify which one you gave more attention to in your drawing. Which one has more color, details?

3. Where do you feel charged, resistant, angered, or triggered?

4. What color is the emotion?

5. Use line, shape, and color to draw out your resistance, limiting belief, anger, or trigger.

NOTE: Be compassionate with yourself. A part of experiencing contrast in life is being able to learn the lesson.

QUESTIONS FOR REFLECTION: What realization came up for you? What do you need to let go of to bring in your attention to your desire? Have you been trapped by your *ego*, trying to protect you? Are you "playing small"? If a person triggered you, identify what parts of their personality bother you. Do you see it in yourself? Now, identify the positive aspects of this person. Do you see that in yourself as well?

Manifesting Art Exercises: Solar Plexus Chakra

1. TITLE: COOL YOU

BENEFITS: Increases self-confidence

RELIEF: Releasing doubt

PREP TIME: 10 minutes

ACTIVITY TIME: 50 minutes

MATERIALS:
- Journal
- Collage materials (magazines, Internet images)
- Glue
- Scissors

ACTIVITY HEADNOTE: Looking at the past to celebrate the now. *What do I have to do to feel more worthy?* Make a list of all the cool things that you have done in your life. I think it was cool my art was on a billboard during 2017 Art Basel in Miami. I got to exhibit and sell my brain-painting collection for three years at a neurosurgeon conference. I met my husband 20 years ago after a psychic told me I was about to meet him (described him perfectly)—and I did!

STEPS:

1. List out all the cool manifestations that have happened in your life that have brought you joy.

2. Choose a few to create a collage.

3. Get out of your comfort zone, and ask a friend what they appreciate about you.

NOTE: We all have unique experiences in our lives. Find how these experiences shaped you.

QUESTIONS FOR REFLECTION: What are your strengths? You are so unique. These experiences shape you into who you are today.

2. ALIGNED ACTION

BENEFITS: Increases self-awareness and emotional resilience, identifies strengths

RELIEF: Decreases doubt because you are taking action

PREP TIME: 10 minutes

ACTIVITY TIME: 50 minutes

MATERIALS:
- Journal
- Drawing materials

ACTIVITY HEADNOTE: Every area of your life needs attention. This is why it's important to take inventory of where you need to place your energy. Small aligned actions can create big shifts. What do you think you need to do next to level up your life? We are taking aligned action with our manifestation. What is the next best step for moving into creating your dream into a reality? What do you feel inspired to do? Take time today to act "as if," so you can move in the direction of your dreams. If your ideal avatar is a Queen, dressed to the nines, then by all means put on your crown. If your ideal avatar is living on the beach, go ahead and start planning a trip. Take the next step to move you closer. Be bold.

Here is a tip: I meditate in the morning and write my morning pages to find my best next step. This process evolves daily. For example, I meditate in the morning and then clear my thoughts by writing. In my writing, I list three things to do related to my big dream that will get me closer to my desire. Whether it's a simple task like writing an email, picking up supplies, or painting, all are steps moving me forward.

One year, I wanted to take my family on a ski trip. I posted an image of a couple skiing on my vision board. While perusing Amazon, a pair of snow boots appeared in my feed. I bought them—something I would never use in Florida. A week later, my friend who lives in Colorado invited my family to her house to go skiing. It was magical! My dream trip manifested! Even if you don't know the how, just take a step anyway. Play the game. What can you do today to move a step closer to your manifestation?

- You can collect images on Pinterest and create a vision board.
- Want a fit body? Put on your workout gear and a YouTube Zumba video.
- Need a boost for selling your products, art, or service? Post a piece of art for sale on Instagram or Facebook
- If you are manifesting money, take an inventory of your money coming in and going out.
- Clean out your closet. Post an item online for sale from your closet.
- Looking for a romantic partner? Pick out an awesome dress for your next date night. What is the feeling you have when you have manifested your desire?
- Do more of the things that result in feelings that make you feel aligned to your desires. Here are some examples I like to do: Buy myself flowers (beauty), meditate (clarity), go roller skating (feeling of freedom), give a compliment (brings appreciation), journal what I'm grateful for (brings abundance).

Life is your masterpiece! Creativity is how we infuse love into everything we do. It's how you decorate your space, cook your dinner, and nurture your relationships.

STEPS:

1. Identify what area of your life that, if you focused attention on it, would have a ripple effect in all other areas.

2. Choose three baby steps to take you closer to your dream.

3. Write it in your planner.

4. Act "as if" it was already here (dress up as the successful artist, go test drive your favorite car, spend the day doing what lights you up).

QUESTIONS FOR REFLECTION: How did it feel to move forward with your vision? Were you uncomfortable or fearful? Was it fun? Continue bringing this emotion of pulling your desire into your life. In what other ways can you bring in the feeling?

3. BUILDING YOUR WILLPOWER

BENEFITS: Increases self-awareness and emotional resilience, identifies strengths

RELIEF: Offers organizational tools for clarity and overcoming obstacles

PREP TIME: 10 minutes

ACTIVITY TIME: 50 minutes

MATERIALS:
- Journal
- Planner (online or paper format)

ACTIVITY HEADNOTE: Everything in life is a choice. I love how Jen Mazer mentions in the interview that you can't make the wrong choice. As you are moving into your power, you can feel it in your body if you're making a decision related to empowering you. Be sensitive to how it feels in your body. Are you leaning in? Does it feel exciting? Do you feel expansive? Moving into your power to reframe how you have to do something, you choose to do something. You move forward even if there is fear involved. The Ego will try to protect you by "playing small." It's important to understand that fear can help you level up your life. I was terrified of posting my art on the Internet. The first time I posted on social media, I went and hid under the covers. That brought back a terrible college critique from a past professor, mentioning I was a turtle in my shell. They were telling me the truth. Yet, in time, I learned that I didn't need people's approval to do what I love. I just share it because it makes me happy. I no longer needed to hide.

STEPS:

1. Weekly planning of desire.

2. Choose Sunday to sit down and write out what needs to get done for the upcoming week. Examples include meeting with your accountability partner, coach, team, supports, or connecting with uplifters.

3. Use the chart below to identify your most urgent/important tasks.

4. Be sure to include self-care time, as it's an important ingredient in manifesting

CHART	
Urgent	Important
Not Urgent	Not Important

QUESTIONS FOR REFLECTION: If any obstacles come up, such as a limiting belief, draw them out in your journal. What does the obstacle look like? For example: the fear of writing the email to your favorite artist that you want to connect with. Draw out the emotion, fear. It's important to handle the obstacles head on. Once you have drawn it out, tear it up, or, even better, burn it. Do you feel you're moving toward your purpose in the world?

Action

Take action towards your desires. What is one area where it would create the biggest ripple effect in your life? Baby steps everyday can lead to a major shift. What is one step you can take today to make your dreams a reality?

Chapter 6

SACRAL CHAKRA

Focus: Letting Go to Let Joy In

The sacral Chakra is about pleasure, sexuality, desires, and emotions. In Sanskrit, it's known as *svadhisttana*; it's located just below the navel. The color frequency related to this Chakra is orange. The intention of this Chakra is to let go and create flow. Hence, the element of this Chakra is water. Our focus will be on letting go and choosing joy. This is about letting go of things, situations, or people that no longer serve you. We are exploring everything that lights you up so you can enjoy the journey. Let's get into the flow to bring us movement, pleasure, change, and growth.

BALANCED ENERGY: When the sacral Chakra is balanced, it will be pleasurable to be sensual, sexual, to nurture and be nurtured. Freud defined The Pleasure Principle: We have a natural inclination to move toward pleasure and away from pain. We look for fulfillment. It can be harmful if we have excessive behaviors such as spending money on frivolous things, drinking too much alcohol, or an addiction to sex. We want to open the Chakra but not become attached. Pleasure is a good thing as long as it's balanced. The sacral Chakra is about satisfying desires and the feeling of joy.

This is a wonderful time to start thinking about what you need to do to let go in order to let your dreams come in and manifest.

IMBALANCED ENERGY: impotence, frigidity, irritable bowel syndrome, kidney stones, uterine, bladder or kidney trouble, stiff lower back (ovaries, testicles), ovarian cancer in women or testicular cancer in men, addictions, shame, and guilt.

When the Chakra is spinning too fast, it's because a person is seeking too much fulfillment from outside influences such as excessive drinking, shopping, or any other addictive behaviors. When the Chakra is spinning too slow, it's because we aren't allowing ourselves to experience joy. Joy is blocked by the feeling of guilt. Do you feel guilty for having a desire?

LOCATION: In the lower abdomen, sacral plexus, seat of life, related to the female's womb.

BODY: This Chakra relates to bodily functions having to do with liquid: circulation of blood, urinary elimination, sexuality, and reproduction, and qualities of water such as flow, formlessness, fluidity, and surrender.

FUNCTION: Expressing needs: emotional and sexual. Divine principle: sensual desire, reproduction, responding, giving and receiving empathy.

ELEMENT: Water

SYMBOLS: Moon, personal pleasures, six-petal lotus, yin and yang, fish, sea creatures, water.

COLOR FREQUENCY: Orange

I remember when my children were young, and I was experiencing bouts of anxiety and depression. We had a home, our heath, and work. Yet, I was missing a key ingredient of creating art for my soul. It left me feeling overwhelmed. I actually felt guilty for asking for "more" in my life. When I realized that what I really wanted was a bigger home with a studio and time to make art, I learned how to let go of the guilt. It was the realization that it's natural to want things—it's in our nature. Desires are essential for moving us forward and experiencing life. When you listen to your soul, it will give you the opportunity to have more joy and live more fully.

This Chakra is about letting go. Yet, when we have resistance in our lives with certain emotions, then we need to take time to dive deeper into the feeling. Do not bypass, which is trying to feel good and ignore the feeling that needs to be addressed. There is a lesson to be learned. In my interview with Lana Shlafer, she recommends honoring where you are and receiving the gift in the pain. She described the emotion scale from Abraham Hicks as a fluid musical chart, moving from one chord (emotion), high notes to low tones. It's important to realize that there is no judgment of the emotion. Do not label an emotion as "good" because it's "positive"; don't label an emotion as "bad" because it's "negative" because it doesn't feel as good. It's being present with the emotion, receiving the gift in the experience of it. As you do this, it will release itself. Well, you might be thinking, "How do you do this? How do you embrace it?" Honoring the emotion is identifying it first, and then creating art about it. This is one of the healing exercises for this Chakra.

Release what no longer serves you.

AFFIRMATIONS:

I am creative and adaptable.
I am sensual and sexual.
I am able to enjoy the pleasures in life.
My emotions are my most intimate ally.

In this interview with Laura Hollick, we are discussing ways to tap into joy and abundance through self-care and your art practice. Laura has lived a beautiful example of this creative practice in her life.

Interview with Laura Hollick:

Laura Hollick is an award-winning artist and visionary guide known as a *Soul Artist*. After walking 10,000 km on a Vision Quest, Laura clarified her purpose and dove into business to realize it. She founded Soul Art Studio Inc. as a way to circulate love around the planet with pure inspiration.

BRAVO TV created a documentary about Laura's art and life called "The Artist's Life—Laura Hollick." She has hosted and produced more than 500 radio shows for 93.3 FM CFMU called "The Artist's Lifestyle." Laura recently gave a TEDx talk called "You Are the Art."

Laura's Soul Art has touched audiences around the globe through her Soul Art Certification program, public art projects like the "Rainbow House," and global events like International Soul Art Day, the Icon Global Vision Quest, and the Yoni Art Project.

www.laurahollick.com

LEAH: How do you define abundance?

LAURA: My idea of abundance is about being able to live out my imagination. It's about being the person I want to be. Abundance is about living the way that I want to live and spending my time doing the things I want to do. It's about being able to fully express and embody who I am.

LEAH: How do you view your art?

LAURA: When I think about art, entrepreneurship, and abundance, it's about being the person you dream of being. It's where you get to feel what your essence is. I know it's not just a painting on the wall. It's your life, and your life is art.

LEAH: What are some daily self-care practices that you use to tap into listening to your intuition?

LAURA: I practice self-care double the amount of time I create art so that I feel full, nourished, and able to come from a full well. People know me as the self-care queen. I'm into nutrition, juicing, and dry-brush massage, and I love my sauna. Without self-care, it's easy to get exhausted and feel like you're pushing rather than expanding.

LEAH: How do you use your diet and what you consume to align with your practice?

LAURA: As artists, we are channels. As creative beings, we channel meaning; there's some kind of inspiration, energy, vision, idea, impulse coming through, but all you've got is your body for it to come through. So if your body's clogged up with limiting beliefs, residue from a meal from two weeks ago, it's going to be hard to channel through. It's like being spiritually bloated when the body is blocked, because things can't get through. I care for my body like it's an athletic pursuit, because the health of my body is my artist's channel. I love green juices, green leafy salads, fruits, and vegetables—the whole rainbow of it all. Nutrition is a big passion of mine.

LEAH: How do you embody trauma and relate it to nutrition?

LAURA: I haven't met anyone who hasn't experienced trauma. I know I certainly have. Trauma causes us to disembody, jump out, and protect ourselves. When we do that, we go into spirit land, where it seems safer. It's a really good strategy in the moment, but, over time, that repeated disembodiment weakens our channel and our capacity to fully express ourselves in our lives.

So, the process of embodiment is the practice of coming back into our body and finding safety. I use nutrition to cultivate that sacred space in my body for my spirit to embody. I eat in ways that keep my body clean, clear, and capable of holding me.

LEAH: How do you digest your day?

LAURA: Every day before I go to sleep, I journal, so that I don't have any undigested residue from the day. If I'm angry, I've processed it, so that I can understand it and care for myself through it. Or, if I'm sad, I get to process it so my sleep can replenish me rather than me tossing and turning in the unprocessed feelings. With self-care practices, you can handle more. You have your resources, sharper intuition, and access to insights that help you move through any challenge.

LEAH: What is wealth, and how do you measure it?

LAURA: Wealth to me is about being in dialogue with the truth of who I am and showing up as that person. Sometimes showing up means focusing on money to create a sense of independence, sovereignty, and personal ownership of my life. But wealth exceeds money. Wealth is a way of being. I measure it by how much I'm being and becoming myself in the world.

LEAH: How about money lessons?

LAURA: Money brings up a lot of wounds, like the little child in us. We're like, "Oh, my gosh—is someone going to take care of me? I have to take care of myself. What if it goes wrong? What if I can't do it? I'm a failure." Money brings up fear, survival, threat, disconnection, isolation, codependency. But money is also a huge spiritual teacher. Money is one of my most respected spirit guides. I have learned a lot about my wounds through money. I've exercised a lot of courage and strength through my journey with money. Money brings up what we are and shows us how we're connecting and interconnecting in the world with other humans.

LEAH: How did you get help with your blocks and learning about money?

LAURA: My art and my creative process are the number-one place I go to for alchemizing blocks. Spending time in nature and listening to my own instincts are powerful practices, too. Of course, I love learning from others, too, but, ultimately, whatever I learn runs through the filter of my own creative spirit, so I have a sense of understanding, and I feel the transformation happening through me.

Strengthening Techniques for the Sacral Chakra:

1. Go to the beach or cleanse yourself with salt. You can pour saltwater over your body in the shower or take a salt bath.

2. Surround yourself with the color orange. You can wear the color orange or paint a wall in your home. Orange is optimism, fun, adventure, and creativity. It's related to the sacral Chakra. A balanced Chakra brings feelings of joy, and an imbalanced Chakra brings feelings of guilt.

3. Eat oranges and carrots.

4. Carry the stone: Coral, Carnelian.

5. Essential Oils: Sweet Orange, Tangerine, Patchouli, Helichrysum

6. Practice more joy. Give yourself time every day to do something you love.

Healing Art Exercises: Sacral Chakra

1. SACRAL CHAKRA MANDALA

BENEFITS: Increases self-awareness and emotional resilience, identifies strengths

RELIEF: Anxiety, Depression, PTSD

PREP TIME: 10 minutes

ACTIVITY TIME: 50 minutes

MATERIALS:
- Journal
- Meditation link: https://leahguzman.com/resource-guide
- Pencil
- Assorted drawing media: Colored pencils, gel pens, or markers (various shades of orange and gold)
- Black-ink pen

ACTIVITY HEADNOTE: This Chakra is about letting go what no longer serves you in order to allow more joy into your life. As you create the mandala, keep in mind what it is that you are desiring. Include the feelings and symbols.

STEPS:

1. Start with the sacral Chakra meditation.
2. Draw a circle with a pencil.
3. Draw another circle around the first circle.
4. Write things you wish to release in between the two circles.
5. Add the six-petal lotus to your design.
6. Continue to add details.
7. Add the Chakra healing colors of various shades of orange.
8. Use the black-ink pen to outline.
9. Add the affirmations that resonate with you: *I let go of guilt. I forgive myself. I let go of what no longer serves me. I am opening myself to joy. I AM OPEN to receive.*

QUESTIONS FOR REFLECTION: In what area of your life are you already abundant? If you would like to increase an area of abundance, look at what is already working for you. Where can you find more joy to bring expansiveness?

2. SACRAL CHAKRA PAINTING WITH SYMBOLS

BENEFITS: Increases self-awareness, emotional resilience, identifies strengths

RELIEF: Release emotions, learn to surrender

PREP TIME: 10 minutes

ACTIVITY TIME: 50 minutes

MATERIALS:
- Small canvas (4" x 4" or 6" x 6")
- Pencil
- Acrylic paint
- Brushes
- Paint palette
- Water container
- Paper towel
- Black pen (fine-point marker)

ACTIVITY HEADNOTE: The sacral Chakra is about a sense of abundance, pleasure, and receptivity. Are you allowing yourself to receive? Let's hit the easy button. Surrendering and receiving is feminine energy. When I started my creative business, I had so much masculine energy. I thought I had to constantly be doing something. When we allow ourselves the self-care and to surrender, we can be receptive to The Universe's gifts. When I was able to relax and listen, The Universe would guide me. There was no longer a struggle or overworking—it was allowing and being in the flow.

STEPS:

1. Choose an image from the Internet for the sacral Chakra. Symbols: moon, tiger, frog, crocodile, dolphin, ocean, fish, stag. You can also choose a symbol that brings you joy or something related to your desire.

2. Draw a circle.

3. Sketch out design on canvas.

4. Use the color orange predominantly in the painting for the outside circle (you can add other colors such as blue for the water).

5. Block in colors.

6. Once the canvas is dry, add affirmations to painting.

NOTE: Hang together with the other Chakras to create a set.

QUESTIONS FOR REFLECTION: Is there an area of your life that feels forced? How can you increase your self-care this week?

3. LETTING GO TO CREATE SPACE

BENEFITS: Increases self-awareness and emotional resilience

RELIEF: Surrendering, removing clutter

PREP TIME: 10 minutes

ACTIVITY TIME: 50 minutes

MATERIALS:
- Journal
- Assorted drawing materials

ACTIVITY HEADNOTE: Write out what you would like to let go of in your life: fears, negativity, hurts, bad habits, relationships that do not serve you. It's important to take inventory of our environment—cluttered closets, unhealthy relationships, or harmful habits—to see how we spend our energy and if it's serving us. Living in a cluttered space actually tires the mind. The Universe prefers order, and so does your mind. When we clean up our environment, let go of objects, and assess our relationships, then we can create space for more of what lights you up.

STEPS:

1. On a sheet of paper, draw a line down the middle.

2. On the left, make a list of what you no longer accept in your life.

3. On the right, list what is necessary in your life.

4. On the side of items you no longer accept, rip up the pieces, and throw them away.

NOTE: You can symbolically let go of what no longer serves you by clearing space in your home. Consider a catch-all drawer, a closet, your desk, or garage.

QUESTIONS FOR REFLECTION: What do you blame yourself for? Let go of disappointment; accept reality. Release all blame and guilt within you. Forgive yourself. Guilt blocks this Chakra.

Manifesting Art Exercises: Sacral Chakra

1. HONOR THE EMOTION

BENEFITS: Increases self-awareness and emotional resilience, identifies strengths

RELIEF: Processing the emotion that is currently being felt through making art.

PREP TIME: 10 minutes

ACTIVITY TIME: 50 minutes

MATERIALS:
- Journal
- Markers
- Colored pencils
- Pens

ACTIVITY HEADNOTE: *Honoring Where You're At* is about naming the feeling. The goal here is not to move away from experiencing the range of emotions. The intention is to feel it and honor it. We want to receive the gift in its message to us. We have a tendency to look at negative emotions as a bad thing, constantly trying not to feel, and disassociate with our pain. I love how Lana Shlafer addresses this in her interview about finding the gift in the pain. Life is about experiencing all emotions, embracing them. We can't live in high vibe 24/7. Yet, we can allow ourselves to be where we are and experience our life with more compassion. The chart below is adapted from Esther Hick's book *Ask, and You Will Receive*.

STEPS:

1. Choose the feeling from the chart of where you are at this moment.

2. Choose a color.

3. Draw a circle.

4. Use line, shape, and color to create the feeling inside the circle.

> *Joy-Appreciation-Empowered-Love-Passion-Enthusiasm-Eagerness-Happiness-Positive expectation-Belief-Optmism-Hopefulness-Contentment-Boredom-Pessimism-Frustration-Impatience-Overwhelmed-Disappoinment-Doubt-Worry-Blame-Discouragment-Anger-Revenge-Hatred-Rage-Jealousy-Insecurity-Guilt-Unworthiness-Fear-Grief-Desperation-Powerlessness*

QUESTIONS FOR REFLECTION: Where are you on the emotional scale? How did you feel before creating art versus afterwards? What is the gift in this feeling for you? What has it taught you?

2. CONTRAST IS CRUCIAL

BENEFITS: Increases self-awareness, emotional resilience, and problem-solving skills

RELIEF: Finding the lesson in the contrast

PREP TIME: 10 minutes

ACTIVITY TIME: 50 minutes

MATERIALS:
- Journal
- Assorted drawing materials

ACTIVITY HEADNOTE: I loved Flora Bowley's interview, where she discussed how contrast is crucial. It's what makes the painting pop. It's where we learn our lessons in the darkness. It's a part of life to experience what we don't want. You have so much power to actively choose what makes you happy. How can you make something you dread more fun? I once had to see art therapy students in an unhealthy environment (imagine a moldy closet). I had to think outside the box (literally), and I chose to start painting murals on the outside walls of the school. I had to use my own will and problem-solving skills to bring more joy to the situation. It was fun! In challenging times, this can help you "flip the script."

STEPS:

1. Identify an area of your life in which you are struggling.

2. Draw out ways you can "flip the script."

3. You can draw this in your journal.

4. Use assorted colors to block it in.

NOTE: This is also an opportunity to ask Source about a way to see light in the situation. Ask for guidance.

QUESTIONS FOR REFLECTION: How does it feel to gain a new perspective on a situation?

3. JOY IS THE KEY

BENEFITS: Increases self-awareness and emotional resilience, and identifies strengths

RELIEF: Relieves stress

PREP TIME: 10 minutes

ACTIVITY TIME: 50 minutes

MATERIALS:
- Assorted drawing materials
- Journal

ACTIVITY HEADNOTE: Learning how to have fun and be playful is the key to manifesting. As we move through the heavy emotions, choose things that bring joy. We can also laugh and not take life so seriously. Manifesting should be easy. Can we just hit the easy button more often in our day? Yes, we are taking aligned action. Let's have fun while we do it. Enlightenment literally means to *lighten up*. The aligned action energy is masculine, while the receiving energy is feminine. It's a balance of doing and allowing. Where can you allow more play into your life? When I go into my studio, I make it a play session by putting on some dance music. I like to document it that way, too. Joy is an expander, and it attracts things to you (clients, money, happiness, friendships, and love). You have the opportunity to create your reality with passion. Use the playful energy to do this. I like to relate this energy to self-care. For us to really enjoy life, we need to take care of our own needs and wants. This exercise identifies areas where we can lighten up in our lives.

STEPS:

1. Identify all personal pleasures you enjoy. Make a list of things that light you up.

2. Now bring this "happiness" energy into your life.

3. This may be a self-care activity.

4. Use assorted drawing materials to create an image, including how you will lighten up.

5. Do something today that brings you joy. We are creating the feeling within us that matches the vibration we want to manifest.

NOTE: For example, if you desire closer friendships, go ahead and start the process. What would you do with your new friends? Have a dance party? Cook them a meal? Draw this out. Then, do the particular activity for yourself. This is an opportunity to bring the energy that you attract to you now.

QUESTIONS FOR REFLECTION: Think back to when you were a child and to other, different stages in your life. What do you love? Anything creative: cooking, gardening, writing, playing in what you love? Write down all the things that would bring a smile to your face. I like to buy myself flowers. How does it feel to nurture yourself? How does it feel to make self-care a priority? You can incorporate this practice by writing it in your journal as a daily practice. Make your dreams and feeling good a priority. Do you feel guilty for having pleasure? Do you prioritize having fun? Joy is the key in manifesting.

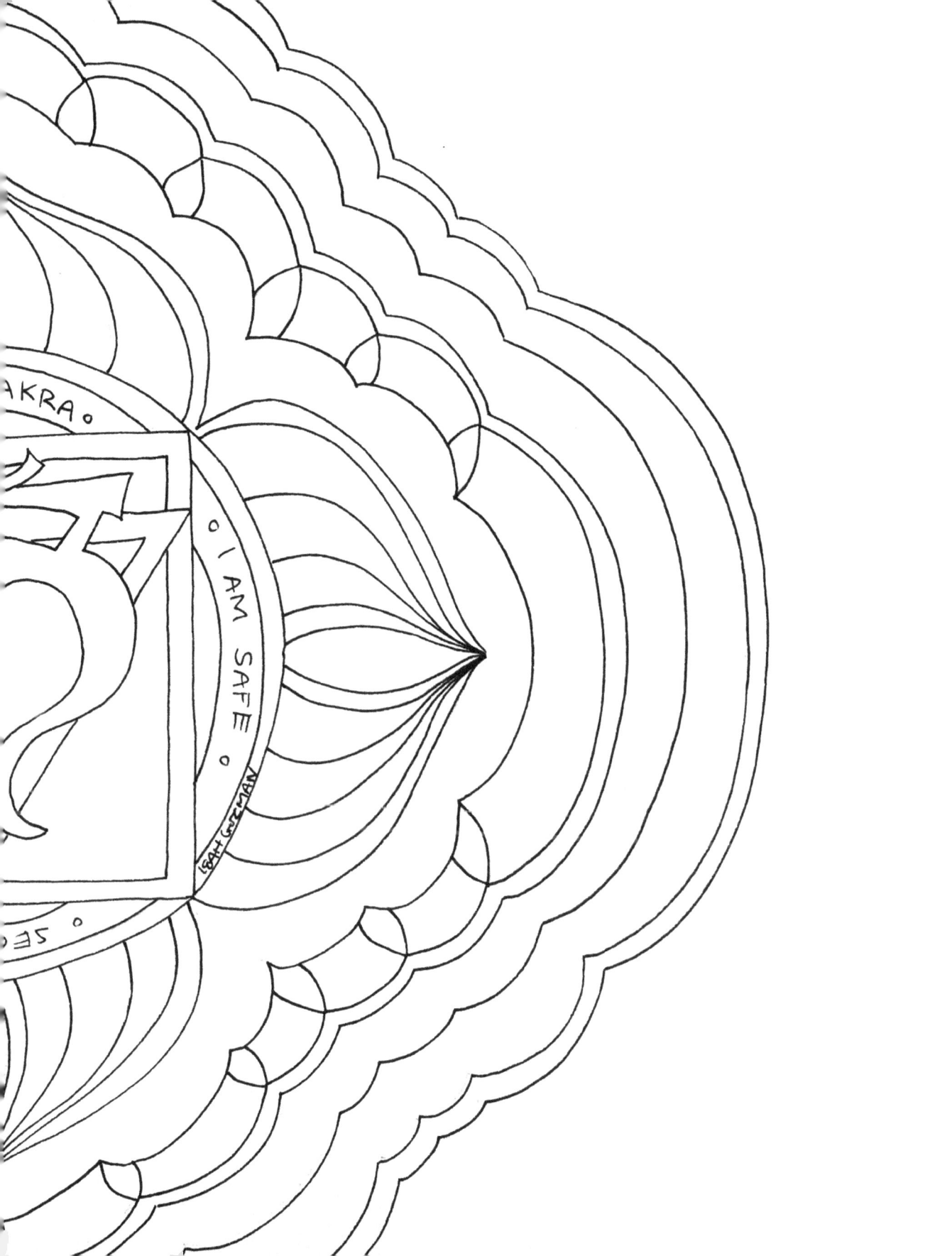

Chapter 7

ROOT CHAKRA

Focus: Surving to Thriving

*T*he root Chakra *is related to the Earth and resonates* at the color frequency of red. In Sanskrit, the root Chakra is known as *muladhara*. This is about feeling safe and secure. It's related to our basic survival needs (food, shelter, water, sleep). It's also connected to your family relationships and to your physical body. According to Hindu philosophy, the purpose of the root Chakra is something to hold onto and create structure. When we relate this to our lives, it's about creating a structure, a platform for our dreams to build on. This structure is related to our daily routines, how we take of our bodies, and how we create success in the balance of our day. If we can create success in one day, it builds into many successful days. The energy around this Chakra is earthy and tribal.

LOCATION: Located at the base of the spine, the pelvic floor, and the first three vertebrae, the root Chakra is responsible for your sense of safety and security on this earthly journey. The Sanskrit word *muladhara* breaks down into *mula,* "root," and *adhara*, which means "support" or "base."

BALANCED ENERGY: The Root Chakra focuses on boundaries, edges, discipline, becoming solidly real, present in the here and now. When your basic needs are met, you feel grounded and safe. Without grounding, we are unstable, we lose our center, and we're unable to manifest our desires. The root is our base structure to build everything upon. We are plugging into ourselves and the earth. What grounds you throughout your day? I prefer morning rituals to ground my day, as well as going barefoot in the grass.

"Whether or not you feel secure now often has less to do with what you have at your disposal and more to do with how safe you felt as a small child. When you consider psychologist Erik Erickson's stages of development, the first stage—trust versus mistrust—is closely related to your root-Chakra development. As infants, if your caregivers readily gave you what you needed to survive, with consistency, you felt secure in the world; you felt that the world was a place that could be trusted to provide your basic needs. Yet, if your caregivers withheld or delayed in giving you what you needed, or if that giving was inconsistent, you may find yourself with first-Chakra blockages." (M. Fondin) I see this in clients who are unable to soothe themselves and lack self-care practices.

FUNCTIONS: Primal state: fight or flight, instinctual; when you're grounded, you have an inner security: power, grace, and peace

ELEMENT: Earth

IMBALANCED ENERGY: An imbalanced root Chakra will make you feel anxious, worried, or fearful. You may experience anxiety disorders, fears, nightmares, weight problems, hemorrhoids, constipation, sciatica, degenerative arthritis, knee troubles, or feet issues. (A. Judith). If the energy is spinning too fast, you may be overly materialistic or have money issues and familial issues. Spinning too slow can show up as insecurity and an inability to trust others. Feelings of anxiety are a sign of an imbalanced root Chakra.

Another feeling associated with an imbalanced root Chakra is fear. Fear triggers the fight-or-flight response. One who is constantly plagued by health problems or is continually struggling with financial crises is caught on the first Chakra level.

Taking care of yourself is a priority. Learn to validate the body, feel it, accept it, and love it. We can respect the natural biorhythms of the body by giving our body nutrition, sleep, and exercise. A nice way to listen to your body is to meditate and then ask, "What do I need to heal the root Chakra?" There are many techniques; choose a few to help you.

> *"Fear has two meanings: Forget Everything and Run or Face Everything and Rise . . . the choice is yours."*
> ~Zig Ziglar

When we aren't operating out of fear, we are more present and available in our lives. Are you hooked up to your source of power and intuition within you, where creative ideas and inspirations flow through? Or are you tuning into fear radio, unavailable to the grace and guidance trying to get in? If so, this is an invitation to step back from the noise, to take a deep breath and hook back up to you. This moment is always about the invitation.

> *"All shallow roots must be uprooted, because they are not deep enough to sustain you."*
> ~A Course in Miracles by Marianne Williamson

SYMBOLS: tree with roots, anchor, elephant (Shiva unblocks obstacles), ox, bull, square, four-petal lotus.

COLOR: Frequency: RED

AFFIRMATIONS:

> I am grounded, safe, and secure.
> I make a good living doing what I love.
> I am stable, strong, and healthy.

In the healing and manifesting exercises for the root Chakra, we are going to address your body, family relationships, structure in your day, and money. All of these are vital for self-care and feeling secure.

From my own experience of suffering from panic attacks in college and resurfacing when I had my children, I know that it can be really uncomfortable to live in the fear mode. It was when I was working full-time as an art therapist and caring for my small children—at the time, they were one and four years old—that I experienced burnout. I had *people pleaser syndrome* as well. I was always saying "Yes" to others. When I realized I had to make a change and get help, a shift occurred. I started prioritizing my big dream. I realized I wanted to be an artist who shares their artwork with the world for public consumption. I also started to realize how the Chakra colors were showing up in my life and my clients' lives as a way to heal. I noticed it in my clients' art, when they were feeling anxious and using the color red to express themselves. As I moved into stepping out by sharing my art with the world, I had to face my fears head on. I had a fear of being judged. I had anxiety about money—that I wasn't making enough. How would I price my work? It was at this time I learned the greatest lessons through my own art practice. I discovered my money monster and how it stemmed from my first experiences with money as an adolescent. I learned to heal my relationship and beliefs by getting intimate with these experiences. By changing my mindset around my relationship and nurturing what I had already. I got to see my garden grow. I started prioritizing my big dream and took baby steps every day to make it happen. I woke up early, at 5:00 a.m., to write one page of this book. I would call in people for support and created my dream to support me. Each day I identified my priorities.

Accountability has been a game changer as well. I like to say it's my secret sauce. Having someone to keep me grounded and reviewing my intentions have taught me to trust myself, because I learned how to follow through with my desires. Do you have someone in your life you can count on to check in with you weekly?

I also learned how to listen to my body as the guidance system that it is. If a new opportunity pops up, how does my body respond? Am I physically leaning in? If I do, that's a "Yes!" If my body has hesitation or uneasiness, then it's a "No." Your body is an instrument to help you determine choices in your life.

Interview with Alena Hennessy:

Alena is the author of *Cultivating Your Creative Life, The Painting Workbook, Intuitive Painting,* and *The Healing Guide to Flower Essences.* She is a beloved teacher of the art-making process, both online and at select retreats. Her work has been featured in numerous magazines and publications. She uses a special *wabi sabi* technique. Her paintings have been exhibited across major cities in the U.S., along with several museum shows. Alena is also a flower-essence practitioner, along with being a Reiki master and energy healer. As a facilitator, her intention is that each participant leave a little more transformed, content, and open to wild possibility.

www.alenahennessy.com

LEAH: Can you tell us more about your journey of being a successful artist, your vision, and how it has taken shape over the years?

ALENA: I've always been an artist. I would spend hours drawing as a kid and went to art school. I unlearned from what I learned in art school. It really just came from life experience and the journey of life itself. Education does help, but I think that unlearning is as important as learning, so you can find your own voice and your own path.

LEAH: Can you tell us about your *wabi sabi* technique?

ALENA: I really appreciate the principles of *wabi sabi*, which are asymmetry and organic beauty. Aged wood is really valued in flower arranging; it relieves the pressure of the piece being a certain way or perfectionism. It encompasses the transitory nature of life, in which everything is always changing, being born, and dying. The process helps students relieve the pressure of the painting being a certain way. There are certain techniques I teach that give way to the creative spirit to be more playful and more curious, and allows the non-cliché and surprises to take place. The process allows the authentic beauty to form, get grounded, less out of the analytical mind and more into your body.

LEAH: How do you teach people to get out of the boundaries and rules we put on ourselves that block our creativity?

ALENA: Centering techniques can really help. I practice warm-up creative exercises. It helps release the ownership of the art (from the learned perception that it needs to be a certain way). Sharing in community is great. Also, find a place within that's untouched by all of these thoughts and ideas. Learning structure and feeling safe in structure. I like to give prompts when I teach so people play, and they can feel freedom within the structure. In art lessons, I find that students need healthy boundaries. It can't be a free-for-all. There is a union of opposites that really works with teaching.

LEAH: Can you tell us about your art practice? Are you someone who paints every day?

ALENA: No, I know there are artists that do that, and it works for them. I'm not one of those people. For me, creativity is a way of life. Everything we're doing, we're doing it with creating, or we're stagnant. I have a cultivated body awareness, a subconscious and self-care awareness. If the day calls for emailing and administrative work, that's going to make me relax more into my creativity. My creativity is something that goes in waves, and I ride that. Deadlines are also a motivation for me that I create for myself. It's really about knowing yourself and what works for you.

LEAH: Do you ever have dry periods when you're not making art?

ALENA: Yes. It's usually because of life circumstances. It might be that I'm going through a big transformation—where something is going to be burned. That happened to me earlier this year. I was in Mexico, and I was going through a big transformation. Big life stuff happened, and I just took a break and slowed it down. Then, when I started to create again, this whole new thing opened up because I had taken a pause. More came out because of the input process. It can be helpful to take away certain things you normally do, change your routine, allow for new inspiration, new patterns, and all the elements coming in. Then, you're like "Wow!" It surprises you, and a whole new series can be born.

LEAH: Have you ever intentionally used art to heal yourself?

ALENA: It has never been the intention or what I sought out, like "Art is going to heal me," or "I need this to heal." It was just something that brought about the effects of dopamine and serotonin that art creates. It came naturally to me, and I know it doesn't come naturally for everyone. I'm more attracted to seeing the impacts it has on people I work with. When we create connection and space for ourselves, that takes time out from the distractions of life and allows time for healing. In my life, the integration I've experienced has come through many different practices such as breathwork, meditation, and taking care of the body-mind connection. Art is the reward; it's the expression. So, energetically getting yourself aligned in whatever way is most important. Art to me is more like honoring life and a way I can be of service to others, how I can be in service of life. Art is like a mirror for each phase of where we're at in our development. It's going to mirror that and magnetizes it.

LEAH: Are you practicing breathwork and meditation daily to help you stay aligned?

ALENA: Absolutely! Even if it's 10 to 20 minutes a day, it will change the quality of your day. Art can be that, too. What is most important is that these self-care practices are infused with each other.

LEAH: I love that I practice every day myself, and, if I don't, I will feel "off." Do you sit down and meditate before you paint?

ALENA: No, I'm usually at the point that I'm really excited to get started and record another lesson. I do like to start and end my day in meditation.

LEAH: Can you tell us about your oracle deck and how it came about?

ALENA: I've really been into oracle decks for a long time. My girlfriends and I would circle up and pull cards for each other. I thought, *I should totally create my own.* I worked on the deck for more than a year and a half. I knew my mom's style would be a good fit, and I was envisioning collaborating with her. We're in our second printing. *Oprah Magazine* called it one of the most beautiful decks out there.

CREATIVE SOUL SOCIETY MEMBER: I'm interested in your journey from college training to your spiritual practice. Were you spiritual before the art-making, and then did the Reiki practice come afterwards?

ALENA: For many years, I did commercial art and sold at trade shows. I sold with galleries, catalogues, and licensing for Urban Outfitters and Papyrus. I was doing work with other people, and then I went through a big life change. I went through a divorce. I got married really young, and I was thinking, *I don't know if this art career is working out for me physically.* It was more wholesale work—it wasn't what my soul wanted. Then, the art world pulled me back in, and I got an amazing opportunity with my first book and a great studio space in Asheville. Then I *knew* I wasn't supposed to leave it. Then I went to a holistic healing program, in which I studied to become a Reiki master, learned flower essence, herbalism, *ayurveda yoga*, and meditation. At the time, I didn't know how I was going to use it and incorporate it into my art career. Then it slowly came together and just started synthesizing. It makes sense now that I look back. Bringing it together has been a real gift. You have the opportunity to create exactly what you want with your soul imprint. I encourage my students to listen and trust. It's like little jigsaw pieces coming together.

LEAH: Do you have any words of wisdom to give artists starting out on their journey of sharing their art with the world?

ALENA: Sharing your work on social media is a really important piece. I found, for instance, a friend who just finished all this training for somatic healing and attachment theory. She's given me a few free sessions, and she's incredible. She's building her website and working part-time. She's stressed out about money. I asked her if she was sharing her new offer on social media, because her community loves her. She wasn't, because she had fears around sharing—it didn't come naturally to her. Anytime we embark on a new path, it's not going to feel natural. It's a new way of being—a new way you haven't done before. The more you share, the more natural it will become. The more she does it, the more it comes from a sincere, authentic place, like asking The Universe for a sign.

Also, ask others to share with anyone you know you're taking new clients. It's valuable to know that it's going to feel scary to feel vulnerable. It will get to the point where it feels really natural, and you'll feel more detached about it—like it's second nature. It's a ride into that uncomfortableness, and that momentum will be building. Just ride into the uncomfortableness, and know that it's natural to feel this way. You're creating a new pathway. The new pathway is going to open up all sorts of worlds for you, and there will be a rhythm that you'll find in that. Trust that it doesn't mean it's not right for you just because it's uncomfortable at the beginning.

We have to remember we all have our own unique genius. There is something that you came here for that is your purpose and gift to other people—no matter what it's like uncovering that genius; we all have it. We can have overlapping geniuses, but then we have something uniquely us. The more that we understand that and nurture it and cultivate it, life tends to reflect back and support you with it.

Additionally, from a soul-evolution perspective, there are certain things that come naturally to us—we're just good at them. What I find is when we give offerings, we need to really understand what comes naturally to us and our wounds. Then, *make your wounds your wisdom*. When you can integrate both of those, it creates the unique genius that is your soul. From that, the offerings have a polarity, the union of opposites. I find this in my own life and other people's lives. I find it very helpful for making sense of life. What we learned through overcoming holds the wisdom. We're all here to grow.

Strengthening Techniques for the Root Chakra:

- Physical exercise: go for a walk, run outside, or practice yoga; connect to your physical body
- Self-care: lotions, oils, baths, time to journal, create a space for *you*
- Practice grounding exercises by being in nature; meditate outside; garden, and get your hands dirty

- Finish any incomplete tasks
- Take care of things you already have (your home, car, yard, relationships)
- Carry the stone in your pocket: Hematite, Bloodstone, Garnet, Red Jasper, Tourmaline, Smoky Quartz, Agate, Tiger's Eye
- Essential Oils: Red Spikenard, Patchouli, Vetiver
- Wear the color red. Red is associated with passion, courage, and excitement. It also relates to the root Chakra. When the Chakra is balanced, you will feel safe, secure, stable; you will see career success. When it's imbalanced, it brings feelings of fear, anxiety, and instability.
- Eat red foods: berries, tomatoes, and proteins

Art Exercises for Healing: Root Chakra

1. ROOT CHAKRA MANDALA

BENEFITS: Increases self-awareness and emotional resilience, identifies strengths

RELIEF: A tool for grounding and alleviating anxiety

PREP TIME: 10 minutes

ACTIVITY TIME: 50 minutes

MATERIALS:
- Journal
- Pencil
- Assorted drawing media: Colored pencils, gel pens, or markers (various shades of red and gold)
- Black-ink pen

ACTIVITY HEADNOTE: The intention for the mandala is to ground you and help you focus. You can start this sacred circle daily as part of your routine or morning pages. It's an opportunity to release and identify what you want to prioritize for the day. What are three baby steps that can take you a little closer to your dream? Be sure to add these to your agenda.

STEPS:

1. Start with the root Chakra meditation. https://leahguzman.com/resource-guide

2. Draw a circle with a pencil.

3. Draw another circle around the first circle.

4. Write affirmations in between the two circles.

5. Add the four-petal lotus to your design.

6. Continue to add details.

7. Add the Chakra healing colors in various shades of red.

8. Use the black-ink pen to outline.

9. Add the affirmations: *I am grounded, safe, and secure. I make a good living doing what I love. I am stable, strong, and healthy.*

NOTE: Even if you didn't complete the priority for the day, don't be hard on yourself. You have tomorrow.

QUESTIONS FOR REFLECTION: Have you considered bringing in an accountability partner? Is there someone in your life who would want to commit to supporting you weekly with your priorities? You could also hire a coach to hold you accountable. Have you established a daily morning practice yet? How you start your day sets the tone. *What are you afraid of? What makes you feel safe and secure?*

2. ROOT CHAKRA PAINTING WITH SYMBOLS

BENEFITS: Increases self-awareness and a visual reminder of your desires

RELIEF: Provides a visual with symbols to help ground your vision

PREP TIME: 10 minutes

ACTIVITY TIME: 50 minutes

MATERIALS:
- Small canvas (4" x 4" or 6" x 6")
- Pencil
- Acrylic paint (white, black, red, silver, or gold)
- Brushes
- Paint palette
- Water container
- Paper towel
- Black pen (fine-point marker)
- Choose a symbol (four-petal lotus, tree with roots, anchor, elephant, ox, snake, lioness, buffalo)
- Look up an image from the internet

ACTIVITY HEADNOTE: Creating the root Chakra symbol painting gives you the opportunity to use the animal symbols, color, and your affirmations as visual reminders of your safety, protection, and resources in your life. By now, you will have a full set of your Chakra art that can be hung and that will bring alignment. You can choose whichever symbol resonates with you for this painting. I have painted the tree with roots, representing a money tree, when I was healing my anxiety around money. I've painted an elephant to represent leadership of a tribe. Choose the symbol that resonates with you. The root Chakra painting is symbolic to commit to recommit. If we lose our momentum and don't complete the tasks related to each of our desires, it will not manifest in your reality. This is a reminder to complete and follow through with your intention.

STEPS:

1. Choose an image from the internet or a symbol to use as inspiration (elephant, tree with roots, four-petal lotus).

2. Draw a circle on canvas.

3. Sketch out the design with your symbol.

4. Use the color red for the outside of the circle or predominantly on the canvas.

5. Block in colors of your sketch.

6. Once the canvas is dry, outline symbols, and add affirmations.

NOTE: Hang this painting with the rest of your Chakra set. It is now complete—infused with intentions to Manifest Your Desire!

QUESTIONS FOR REFLECTION: Where do you need to step up, finish, or fully commit yourself? Are you prioritizing your desires into your calendar? Choose three things today you will do to take the next step. Find a partner to hold you accountable.

3. MONEY MONSTER

ART: Artwork by an art-therapy client of Leah Guzman

BENEFITS: Increases money awareness

RELIEF: Anxiety from money issues

PREP TIME: 10 minutes

ACTIVITY TIME: 50 minutes

MATERIALS:
- Journal
- Assorted drawing materials (colored pencils, pens, and markers)

ACTIVITY HEADNOTE: Abundance is all around us. This exercise gives you an opportunity to see what your relationship is to your beliefs around money. How does money make you feel? Do you feel abundant? Or does money make you feel anxious? Are you energetically pushing it away? People do this all the time and are not realizing their actions. This exercise helps you discover your relationship with money. Below are some common ways that we push money away from us.

Actions That Block Abundance

Sometimes we have an unconscious connection. The purpose of this exercise is to see our underlying relationship with money, and become more aware of our actions and conscious of what we do with it.

Actions that block money flowing to you:

- Words we speak (*I can't afford this. I never have enough*)
- Not being open to receive (not accepting compliments, gifts, money)
- Neediness (never enough)
- Anxiety (related to pricing work, charging for service)
- Not feeling worthy
- Money is evil (belief)
- Avoid looking at bills (bank statements, balancing accounts)

Common beliefs that block abundance coming to you:

- If I have more, then someone else has less.
- I have to work hard to make money.
- You have to be born into money.
- Bad people have the most money (people in power).
- Money goes out as fast as it comes in.
- Money is the root of all evil.
- There's not enough to go around.
- I'm not good with money.
- I'm not good enough.

s hard to come by. People in my family arent good at making money. People in my family arent good enough to make money. Creativity isnt always... people will rip you off and they are... rich people are not... rich people are greedy and selfish. Money is scarce and must be worked hard for and is still hard to come by... be broke. Money is the... evil. It's stupid to spend money... not having money gives... an @ives... heavy impossible... one taught me about how to make money...

- I'm not smart enough to be rich.
- People will judge me for having money.
- Resentment for not making enough.
- Feeling guilty for wanting more.

STEPS:

1. Write in your journal what your first experience was with money as a child.

2. Write in your journal what your first negative experience associated with money was as you were growing up.

3. Visualization: Close your eyes. Imagine yourself as a child. You're with one of your parents. Pick a specific place in your house. What are your parent(s) doing? What does it smell like? What does it look like? What are you doing? Think about all the things they said about money and attitudes about money.

4. Write down the primary beliefs you got from each parent about money. Circle one that is strongest for you. This is your limiting "belief."

5. What were your beliefs that were created from these experiences?

6. Use assorted drawing materials to draw out your own money monster.

7. Include feeling in your image. You are drawing out your relationship with money.

8. Include any limiting beliefs associated with how you view money in your life.

NOTE: If this brings up too much anxiety, I recommend seeking support in this area of your life.

QUESTIONS FOR REFLECTION: What message does your money monster have for you? Focus on your finances. Schedule a money date. Review all finances coming in and going out. See where you will save, invest, and spend. Place your money date on the calendar to review weekly. If this is causing anxiety for you, you can practice rituals to make your date more fun. You can have your favorite beverage and chocolate. I recommend doing the money dates and healing for yourself first. When you feel empowered and know what is coming in and going out, then sit with your partner to plan.

Manifesting Art Exercises: Root Chakra

1. MONEY HONEY

ART: Created by an art-therapy client of Leah Guzman

BENEFITS: Increases wealth consciousness and growth mindset

RELIEF: Anxiety around finances

PREP TIME: 10 minutes

ACTIVITY TIME: 50 minutes

MATERIALS:
- Journal
- Markers
- Colored pencils

ACTIVITY HEADNOTE: The Money Honey is tapping into wealth consciousness. This exercise will help heal the anxiety around money and will change the story that blocks us from tapping into the Universal Flow—the one that says that there is enough for you and everyone else. This is one of my favorite exercises to do with clients. In the image provided, my client created their money monster first and then tapped into their Money Honey. This can be a drawing of yourself or a fictional character. What I loved about this image is that my client had also wanted to manifest not only more money but also a lover. A few months after creating this image, she not only healed her money story but also manifested a lover who looked just like this image! I couldn't believe the similarities. She let me know he was also helping her have a better relationship with her finances.

STEPS:

1. What does abundance look like for you?

2. Create an image of your Money Honey. It can be a person or something symbolizing an abundance of money for you.

3. Add other items to symbolize wealth consciousness (money, honey, abundance overflowing)

4. Add money-manifesting affirmations: *Money flows easily to me. I make more than _____ a month. I love money, and money loves me. My clients love paying me, and I love receiving money from them!*

NOTE:
- Use your imagination to get into the abundance mindset.
- How would it be different for you in your life if you could live beyond your limiting beliefs?
- What would be different?
- What would you do or stop doing?
- How much will each desire cost? (Research your answers.)
- How much do you want to make this coming year?
- Double it.

AFFIRMATIONS TO BUILD YOUR MONEY MINDSET:
- Money flows easily to me from many different sources.
- It's easy for me to make money.
- I'm worthy of large amounts of money.
- I can do good things with my money.
- Money is a powerful tool that can help me and others.
- I make wise choices with my money.
- I have complete control over my finances.
- My clients pay me well and on time.
- Wealthy people are good and honest.
- Money is pouring into my reality.

- Money comes to me from known and unknown sources.
- Money is easy to make as I have fun helping people.
- I attract clients who are happy to give me money.

QUESTIONS FOR REFLECTION: What message does your art have? Learn to love your relationship with money. Be open to receiving money from different places. Brainstorm 10 crazy, brilliant ways to make money. Examples include: raise your rates, get a roommate, invest in stocks, get a loan, sell things from your closet on eBay, create an online program (this can be addicting). Tap into Source: Ask, *What is the next best step to bring in money?*

2. STRUCTURING SUCCESS

BENEFITS: Increases self-awareness and emotional resilience, identifies strengths

RELIEF: Provides a plan for unfinished tasks

PREP TIME: 10 minutes

ACTIVITY TIME: 50 minutes

MATERIALS:
- Focus wheel completed from the crown Chakra
- Agenda

ACTIVITY HEADNOTE: Structuring success is a balance of your relationships with self, partner, work, money, home, and family. Grounding your desires is taking baby steps every day to make your dream come true. If you get off track, commit to recommit. Create a game plan; execute it in small chunks. Give yourself a due date for completion. Follow through. The Universe rewards completed actions.

STEPS:

1. Create a consistent schedule.

2. Use an agenda and plan out tasks the week before.

3. Take baby steps daily toward your desires.

4. Congratulate yourself for tracking and following through.

5. Celebrate! Happy dance.

QUESTIONS FOR REFLECTION: Review your focus wheel from the Crown Chakra Manifesting Exercise. Have your numbers shifted? If you need to commit or focus your attention somewhere else, use it as your gauge. How are you showing up for yourself? How are you taking care of your energy? For the commitments that you followed through on and increased in number, celebrate your success! Yes, do a happy dance!

3. EMBODY THE VISION

ART: Photo by Leah Guzman

BENEFITS: Reminds you to take steps to your big dream daily

RELIEF: Releases doubts

PREP TIME: 10 minutes

ACTIVITY TIME: 50 minutes

MATERIALS:
- Clay
- Journal

ACTIVITY HEADNOTE: The more grounded you are in your day-to-day, the easier it is to manifest what you want in your life. By practicing self-care and nurturing your relationships to people, time, finances, and your body, the more success you will have in this process. If you've been avoiding an area of life that needs to be addressed, I'm giving you permission to address it now.

When we embody our vision, we are bringing it into reality. When I had the vision to create a successful empire, I found the "key" as the symbol and made it my logo. The key symbolically represents supporting my clients connecting to mind, body, and soul, as well as my path of connecting to Source daily for guidance. We are nourished by the Earth (this is why we are using clay in this exercise). We are tapping into embodying our desire and plugging into the support of The Universe.

The first step I took to create my logo was drawing it out in my sketchbook. I then took all my broken gold pieces to a jeweler friend and asked her to create me a necklace as a daily reminder of my *Big Reality*. I knew it would take time and attention to nurture my garden. My *Big Dream* of a Creative Empire is going to take years to see it come to fruition. The process of making a creative empire is the same as life being a masterpiece. Each path I take on this journey, unexpected detours, gardens to tend, cities to explore, and summit I reach are all a part of the adventure. This is an opportunity for you to embody your vision into the physical reality.

STEPS:

1. Practice the grounding meditation.

2. Create a symbol to ground your vision (it may be your business or personal logo).

3. This can start as a simple sketch.

4. Create the sketch into a sculpture.

5. Place your sculpture somewhere you will see it every day. You can even wear it!

QUESTIONS FOR REFLECTION: Congratulations! How are you going to celebrate your journey today?

CONCLUSION: Now that we've made it through to the end, you have an abundant collection of art pieces, tools, and techniques to guide you on your journey of healing. You also have clarity on your path to manifesting your desires. I'm excited to see all your big dreams come true. It's only a matter of time and energy shifts that your big vision will transform into a reality. You've got this! Be sure to share your art, manifestations, and love with me!

ACKNOWLEDGMENTS

I want to thank the amazing creatives, Alena Hennessy, Laura Hollick, Ekaterina Popova, Flora Bowley, Jen Mazer, and Lana Shlafer who are interviewed in this book for your time and wise words. Thank you for being such an amazing light source. I'm so inspired by your practices. I appreciate the 1106 Design team for assisting me with putting this book together. Thank you to the awesome Creative Soul Society Membership and Creative Soul Online retreat communities that continue to nourish my soul. I'm grateful for my amazing husband, Jorge Guzman, who supports and encourages me to share my gifts with the world. Lastly, a great appreciation and shout out to my two magical children, Joaquin and Carmen. You both motivate me to practice what I preach.

What did you learn about yourself in this book? I would love to hear about your amazing manifestations. Please let me know. You can schedule your very own Creative Soul Session to review your insights at https://leahguzman.as.me/?appointmentType=14044142

Let's connect on Instagram:

@leah.guzman.art
@art.therapy.online
@creative.soul.society

Are you looking for more daily inspiration?

ART OF HEALING AND MANIFESTING ORACLE DECK can be used as a way to connect with Source. Each card contains a unique message for you to gain clarity of direction on your journey.

CREATIVE SOUL SOCIETY MEMBERSHIP Monthly Online Group: Meet up to heal and manifest. If you would like to see art-making videos of the exercises in this book, they are recorded for you in the membership portal.

ART OF HEALING AND MANIFESTING PROGRAM: Leah's signature program focuses on personal development. It includes individual art-therapy and coaching sessions. Also, online painting courses, building your creative business, and helping you navigate your next step in transformation.

View art and offerings at www.leahguzman.com

REFERENCES

"To Boost Your Emotional Intelligence, Stop Using This Word Inside Your Head," by Minda Zetlin, Inc. Apple News, January 23, 2021

Super Attractor, Gabrielle Bernstein, Hay House

Manifest That Miracle, Lana Shlafer

Wheel of Life, Anodea Judith

Creating on Purpose, Anodea Judith

Oprah and Deepak Meditation Experience

Creative Visualization, Shakti Gawain

C. Tuttle, videos

"Listen: Heal Your Pain," *Spirituality and Health Magazine*, January/February 2021, Peters, Julie

"What Everyone Needs to Know About Their Chakras," *Mind Body Green*, Chopra, Deepak Dec. 11, 2013

Universeofsymbolism.com/Chakra-animals.html

Ask and It Is Given, Esther Hicks

Source: https://www.ncbi.nlm.nih.gov/pmc/articles/PMC3944420/

https://theconversation.com/brain-research-shows-the-arts-promote-mental-health-136668 https://www.npr.org/sections/health-shots/2020/01/11/795010044/feeling-artsy-heres-how-making-art-helps-your-brain

Brené Brown, *Sacred Wisdom Chart*, Helion Publishing

Announcing the Healthy Mind Platter, The healthy mind platter for optimal brain matter. Posted June 2, 2011, David Bock, *Psychology Today Online*

ABOUT THE AUTHOR

Leah Guzman, ATR-BC, is a professional artist and board-certified art therapist. She supports creatives with healing and manifesting their desires utilizing art media through art-therapy services and coaching.

She has written three art therapy books, an international best seller, *Essential Art Therapy Exercises: Effective Techniques to Manage Anxiety, Depression, and PTSD*, and is the author of a children's book, *Rad Is Smad!*

Her signature program, *Art of Healing and Manifesting*, supports creatives by healing emotional wounds and transforming energy to be their most authentic self. She focuses on the Law of Attraction, spirituality, and cognitive-behavioral art-therapy techniques. She also has other online courses such as the Creative Soul Society, a monthly art-making membership group, and art-as-therapy painting classes on her website.

Leah has a consistent art-making practice. Her art is mixed-media paintings that embody high energy, richness in color, visual harmony, and beauty. She lives in Miami, Florida, with her husband, Jorge, and two beautiful children, Joaquin and Carmen. She received a Bachelor of Fine Arts degree in studio sculpture from Georgia State

University and then studied painting at the San Francisco Art Institute. Later, she earned a Master's degree in Art Therapy at Florida State University and became a Board Certified Art Therapist.

> *"It's an honor to have supported thousands of creatives in finding more joy, wealth, and peace in their lives through my techniques."*
> ~Leah Guzman

www.ingramcontent.com/pod-product-compliance
Lightning Source LLC
Chambersburg PA
CBHW051119110526
44589CB00026B/2977